PRAISE F

Why I Cam

"No writer has done a better job both accommodating his art and defending the wilderness around him than Rick Bass. *Why I Came West* is a generous accounting of the rewards and the price, often spiritual, of that endless battle. Bass is a hero in the American West, and we're all lucky he came."

—DOUG PEACOCK, author of *The Essential Grizzly* and *Walking It Off*

"A beautiful love letter to what remains of the 'last best place' west of the Mississippi."

—HOWARD FRANK MOSHER

"[T]he latest in a creel of satisfying Bass books... as colorfully self-revealing as Ernest Hemingway's *A Moveable Feast*."

—*CHRISTIAN SCIENCE MONITOR*

"A nuanced blend of autobiography and environmental advocacy."

—*KIRKUS REVIEWS*

"Versed in paradox, Bass is bracing in his candor about how difficult it will be to change our destructive ways and incandescent in his reasoned call to preserve the few remaining unspoiled places."

—*BOOKLIST*

Why I Came West

Books by Rick Bass

The Deer Pasture

Wild to the Heart

The Watch

Oil Notes

Winter

The Ninemile Wolves

Platte River

In the Loyal Mountains

The Lost Grizzlies

The Book of Yaak

The Sky, the Stars, the Wilderness

Where the Sea Used to Be

Fiber

The New Wolves

Brown Dog of the Yaak

Colter

The Hermit's Story

The Roadless Yaak (Editor)

Caribou Rising

Falling from Grace in Texas
(Coeditor with Paul Christensen)

The *Diezmo*

The Lives of Rocks

Why I Came West

Rick Bass

Why I Came West

MARINER BOOKS
HOUGHTON MIFFLIN HARCOURT
Boston • New York

First Mariner Books edition 2009

For information about permission to reproduce selections from this book, write to Permissions, Houghton Mifflin Harcourt Publishing Company, 215 Park Avenue South, New York, New York 10003.

www.hmhbooks.com

Library of Congress Cataloging-in-Publication Data

Bass, Rick, date.
Why I came West / Rick Bass.
p. cm.
ISBN 978-0-618-59675-1
ISBN 978-0-547-23771-8 (pbk.)
1. Bass, Rick, date. 2. Bass, Rick, 1958 — Homes and haunts — Montana — Yaak Valley. 3. Authors, American — 20th century — Biography. 4. Authorship. I. Title.
PS3552.A8213Z477 2008
333.78'2'092 — dc22 2007030660

Printed in the United States of America

Book design by Robert Overholtzer

DOC 10 9 8 7 6 5 4 3 2 1

Portions of "Meat" first appeared in *Esquire* and *Wasatch Journal.* Portions of "Landscape and Imagination" first appeared in *Sierra* and *Kenyon Review.* Portions of "Bear Spray Stories" first appeared in *Amicus Journal.* Portions of "The Community of Glaciers" and "The Poison of Language" first appeared in *Audubon.* Portions of "The Question" first appeared in the Patagonia® catalogue. Portions of "Why I Came West" first appeared in *Sundance* newsletter, *West,* and *Wasatch Journal.* Portions of "Threshold" first appeared in *Mother Jones.* Excerpt from "The Swan," from *Winter Hours: Prose, Prose Poems, and Poems* by Mary Oliver. Copyright © 1999 by Mary Oliver. Reprinted by permission of Houghton Mifflin Company. All rights reserved. Recipe for Lobster, Fennel, and Orange Soup from *Bistro Cooking at Home* by Gordon Hamersley and Joanne McAllister Smart, copyright © 2003 by Gordon Hamersley. Used by permission of Broadway Books, a division of Random House, Inc.

For Robyn and Tim

ALWAYS THERE, DAY AND NIGHT,

YEAR AFTER YEAR

Contents

Why I Came West

Introduction

HOW TO BEGIN, where to begin, with a story of love? A conventional beginning would originate with the first sighting, and though as a younger man and a romantic I might have had more tolerance for the unprovable notion that certain loves exist, unmatched, long before the principals intersect with each other, here in middle age I have less patience for such fairy-tale musings. Nonetheless, so immediate was my attraction to the place I now call home — the place where I have lived for the last twenty-one years — that I would be hard put to argue that there might not have always existed a kind of magnetism, operating in either the subterranean earthworks of the layered substrate or in the equally inscrutable celestial arrangement of sky and unseen constellations — the magnetism of planets and black hole gravities exerting a fierce call on the specific directions and probabilities, if not quite the ultimate destinies, of all below — that summoned me from my claustrophobic and uniplanar childhood in the petrochemical redoubt of Houston, Texas, toward the high country of the Rocky Mountain West.

Much as I would like to believe something like that was at work in my life, I still have my doubts, for it seems to imply a mightier importance, that for such foreordination to exist there must be a quite significant relationship between ourselves and the rest of the world. It suggests that in terms or matters of spirit, we may be more important to the world — and the landscape — than we really are. And yet — again, I vacillate — for certain, such predestinies, summonings, and geomagnetisms exist for the wild geese and salmon, for the cranes and wild ducks. So although our own species is much younger and less fitted to the world, less integral and integrated than those more ancient residents, might not similar accommodations, or rather, negotiations, exist for and within us, after all?

It is possible.

It is possible also that there is simply a grand luck in the world, and that I fell privy to it.

It could be posited also that we are shaped and directed by landscape at every turn of our existence — that such sculpting not only occurred in our deeper, more primitive past, but is every bit as ongoing now as it has ever been. We are still such a new species, so late to arrive in the world — in either the Darwinist's or fundamentalist Biblicist's interpretation — that I do not think in the least that our development is completed; hopefully, the species we are now — for better as well as worse — does not represent mankind at the top of our game.

As the workings of a cell are said to match and direct the larger-scale processes of life within the organs, which in turn often mirror the function of the organism itself, so too might the paths of our individual lives represent a course or chart or map of our development as a population, a culture, and even a species.

And even though in our individual lives we can point out our wrong turns and the apparent hopelessness of changing those courses, we can also get back onto the correct path in our larger and developing lives as population, culture, species. I have been lost in the woods enough times to know that you can almost always — eventually — find your way back home. And just as there is a certain mal-ease that attends to the individual traveler when he or she first becomes lost — that uncomfortable sensation in which the body knows it is lost some few moments before the mind, so too, surely, then must there be a similar feeling, some time or distance after the fact, when one gets off the true or best path in the arc toward a population's, a culture's, and even a species' fuller potential.

But I digress, which is what I have always done, for as long as I can remember. There is something in me that prefers — sometimes desperately — to avoid a straight line, and that is stimulated, or maybe even comforted by, disorder and unforeclosed possibility. It is a condition that this amazing landscape, the Yaak Valley of extreme northwest Montana, into which I stumbled some twenty-one years ago, elicits, even nurtures. As I will testify in the coming pages, one of the most powerful and attractive things about this landscape is its duality, its ever-present two-storied-ness. It is not so much yin and yang as something else; it seems to sometimes possess another dimension. Here, more so than anywhere else I have ever been, the presence of one thing does not take away from the ability for other things to be present: a condition as startling as if to discover that, in some places, day does not necessarily come at the expense of night, or that famine is across the cusp from feast. There is a fecundity and a richness here, where the moisture and moderation of the Pacific Northwest weather systems drape themselves across the stony austerity of the northern Rockies. At every level — beginning at the easily quantified and easily observed realms of essence and, I suspect, radiating outward (as well as telescoping downward) into the unseen and immeasurable ones — this richness of spirit, possibility, imagination, and plain otherness permeates.

I digress. I cannot help it. Such discursiveness is often viewed as a southern affliction — indeed, growing up in Texas and then working as an earth diver, a geologist, in Mississippi, I witnessed, and felt immersed in, such a culture of storytelling, in which plot was vastly inferior to a fertility of language as verdant as the landscape, and in which the story often lay as coiled and wild as the unspoken and unacted-upon emotions repressed beneath our time-honored code of manners that was so strictly bounded as to assume a kind of lithology.

But here — this land of blue and white, ice and snow, as opposed to Mississippi's greens and yellows — the Yaak, despite being so wildly Montanan, even physically resembles the South. Because of its low elevation — the lowest in the state, surprisingly, with a reading of 1,880 feet at the confluence of the Yaak and Kootenai rivers — the Yaak rarely gets up above tree line, remaining forested instead (except where clearcuts have gnawed their way across the mountaintops), giving the valley a softer, at times almost velvet appearance.

Further anomalous, and further accentuating that strange initial visual impression of southernness, is the fact that during the retreat of the Ice Age, as the Cordilleran ice shield melted, with the clutching, carving, grasping claws of glaciers sculpting, in that contraction of the dramatic jagged sawteeth that we think of as the typical Rocky Mountain landscapes of rock and ice — shredding the essence of the earth itself, stone, into a vertical tableau of cirque and headwall, cliff and crevasse — the Yaak, being lower, slept a blue sleep beneath seven thousand feet of ice, even as the ice sheets all around the Yaak, including the one overlying the Cabinet Mountains just to the south — just on the other side of the thin and to some extent biologically invisible dividing line of the Kootenai River — thinned quickly to nothing, melting to Pleistocene torrents.

So while the rest of the West was being sawed and shredded, sculpted by teeth and jaws of ice, the Yaak slumbered beneath nearly a mile and a half of ice, like a civilization not yet born. Different destinies and different worlds were dreamed beneath that seven thousand feet of blue ice, while only a few hundred yards away, on the southern side of what would one day be called the Kootenai River, the Cabinet Mountains, ice-scarred, were revealed to the bright light of day and the cold light of the moon; and in them, each day, new life began, or began again.

And when the Yaak did finally emerge, as if refreshed, it did so with softer shapes, with the sediments from the old Belt Sea of nearly a billion years ago having been compressed, like the clay they once were, into the humped and rounded shapes of animals. Much of the Yaak looks more like the Smoky Mountains than what we're accustomed to thinking of as the Rocky Mountain West. It's a southern landscape. It's brimming with vegetation, expansive. It's inviting in some way I can't put a finger on, and it elicits thoughts of seething possibility, fecund unboundedness. Bounty, not paucity. Moisture amid the arid West.

This, again, is yet another of the Yaak's stories, then — to be always at the edge of things (it's the southernmost terminus, as well, of Canada's largest mountain range, the massive Purcell Range) — and yet, again with that Yaakish aspect of duality, the Yaak is also at times at the center of other things. It's the crux and crossroads of the Yellowstone-to-Yukon continuum of that part of North America's wild country that follows the continental divide for some 2,000 miles, and the Yaak is also the vital cornerstone for critical east-west migration of species and genes and populations mixing from the giant Glacier National Park–Bob Marshall ecosystem into the Selkirk Mountains of Idaho, the Colville National Forest of eastern Washington, and, ultimately, Washington's Cascades. The Yaak is also the Northern Rockies' bull's-eye epicenter of larch distribution; this amazing tree — again, two stories — is the West's only deciduous conifer, with one evolutionary foot in the primitive camp of gymnosperms and the other in the more modern company of angiosperms. (In typical contrarian Yaak fashion, the giant larch are the rarest form of old growth in the West, and yet in the Yaak they are the most common form of old growth.)

I didn't know any of this science, didn't know anything, when I first wandered — stumbled — into the Yaak in the green summer of 1987. I just knew that I loved it: that a harmony, and a desire for fit — a deep, biological desire — was struck, in that first sighting, first odor, first touch.

So I can see what has shaped me; I can identify, fairly easily, those forces, images, and impressions toward which I was already disposed, and which have brought richness and complexity to my life, and have — gradually, because I am a slow learner — helped teach me things about natural processes, which have also been helpful in how I look at the rest of the world and my place and goals and manners in that world. Lessons such as the discovery that you can possess seemingly competing and even oppositional ideas, and discoveries such as the notion that you don't have to be perfect in the world, just sensate and passionate, which is sometimes as challenging as perfection. Perfection — in the biological sense — has come slowly to all the other species that have been here so many millions of years longer than we have; how many millions more do we have to wait, and work, and yearn? Surely being sensate and passionate are the first two basic steps across those millions-of-years-yet-to-come.

It will not come in this lifetime.

But what drew me here?

I can identify, fairly easily, those predispositions toward which I was already canted. It's the big question for me, why the Yaak? There are similarities between the South and the Yaak, but there are huge differences, as well — particularly between the loss of individuality, loss of voice, in the suburban, homogenous, petrochemical mall-land of Houston, where I grew up, and the gnarly fecundity of Yaak. I believe strongly that the antithesis of a thing can shape, define, sculpt, the boundaries of the other thing, the thing-to-come; and maybe it was, and is, that simple. Perhaps growing up in Houston is what created in me the place and space for loving — needing — so deeply this rank wild mountain valley so unlike where I was raised.

But how did I come to find this place? What summons first pulled me to it?

Perhaps there had existed always a place and a summons for me here, in which case the question is surely unanswerable — or perhaps the summons began to accrue in parts and portions, in which case I can look back and guess at different pieces that helped assemble and maybe create that beckoning.

My other, older lives, then — as a child in suburban Houston, and, later, an oil and gas geologist wearing a coat and tie and working in a skyscraper, exploring the Southeast for petroleum — are so different from my grittier blue-collar or no-collar life today, of elk hunting, firewood cutting, chain saws, small-town gossip, wildfire, and snowstorms, that it is hard to track any logical path of transition but instead feels like disjointed, disrupted, fragmented sorties and efforts at being in the world. Only until I got to this place and saw, and breathed, the wilderness, did any of that change. And then I saw that wilderness being taken away, disregarded, damaged.

It would be judgmental of me to suggest that of those three lives, any one is more authentic than the other. But I know that in those other lives much of the time I moved through the world as if in a fog of sleep or inattentiveness; that the days were not as often characterized by an over-awareness or attentiveness to the physical senses. Instead I spent a significant amount of time in the interior world — you could call it the dream world, though it was not really so deep as what I would consider for a place described as such.

Instead, it was more just a kind of sleeping or resting, a kind of waiting without realizing that was what I was doing. The days — like any of our days — were punctuated of course by any number of fine and singular and interesting, even exciting, events: but still, looking back now, I can perceive that there was a kind of waiting going on, or a kind of stillness.

And then one day I felt like getting up and moving, stirring, leaving.

What then is the answer to that first question, from which I have digressed so far? Do our personal destinies lie below us, with powerful predispositions, or do they exist more strongly in this world-above, with its scour of wind and ice, its tongues of flame, and all its other magnificent testings and fashionings of our spirit?

I think the answer is an unsatisfying *both:* a unique and authentic, time-crafted land will certainly sculpt your fit to it, but there can also exist a summons — an unseen tendril of logic and grace — of fittedness — that has not yet been achieved but which yearns to be achieved, with every bit as much of the power and unseen subtle elegance of mere electrons and neutrons and protons (if such things even go by those olden names anymore). That as there is a chemistry of soil and stone, so too might there be a chemistry of spirit, a kind of awareness or trembling pre-awareness, even between objects separated by great distances. Much that is "meant" to happen may never happen — in the physical world as well as in this unseen world of spirit and extreme possibility — but as the two atoms, or elements, or characters (a man or a woman, and a landscape, for instance, or two or more of anything) draw closer, then in such a world surely possibility begins to become more winnowed and direct. The world begins to reassemble with greater alacrity (even if it is only that tiny world that exists like a hydrophilic bubble around the traveler, seeking and attracting certain electric charges and rejecting others, with the traveler pulsing on, like a salmon, through a larger world, a sea of such charges and possibilities — a shimmering yet unseen matrix, or fabric, of such charges) as the one element drifts (and is perhaps slightly, ever so slightly, pulled) toward the other.

Possibility, over time, begins instead to resemble something more like order, and then, after a while longer, the increasing order becomes meaning and purpose. The two elements conjoin, and purpose becomes spirit.

Such paths and processes exist in the physical world above; and surely then they exist, even if unseen, in all the other layers and levels of the world.

All of which is to say, the summons, in the beginning, does not have to be large, nor the first step of the journey dramatic. It can be but a whisper, a thought, a question, even a dream.

I've written in other books a superficial or cosmetic description of how we got here — my girlfriend (and later wife), Elizabeth, and me — falling in love with the valley the first second we saw it, and being offered a plum caretaking job the first day we arrived, all but penniless; and about the challenges, at times ludicrous, of adjusting, adapting, from summer in Mississippi — where after college I had been living and working as a geologist — to winter in Montana. Throwing everything in a big yellow rental truck and journeying north and west, once we had landed that miracle (or so it seemed) caretaker position, and limping north, muscling north — flat tires, blown engines in the mountains, dropped transmissions, and so on; in downtown Santa Fe, the car we were towing behind the rental truck slipped free of its trailer hitch and began rolling through town on its own, unpiloted, unrestrained, before coming to rest on the back bumper of another motorist's car, rolling through a red-lit busy intersection on its own, at a slightly different tangent from our direction, as if trying to escape the destination toward which we were traveling. As it was for the white pioneers and their Conestogas, so it remains for all pilgrims in this century and, likely, the next.

But we got here, eventually — just before the first snow — and although each of the twenty-one years has been in its own way as graceless and herky-jerky as the first, I do believe a kind of sanding-down or wearing-down, a shaping, has occurred — like snow falling and pressing down upon the sleeping shapes of things — so that in certain ways, this world, this life, is like those previous dream-lives.

And yet: this one feels more balanced than the others, more grounded. As if — in my inescapable and unavoidable human clumsiness — the physical senses, which are so easily accessible here, help provide a stability, a grounding, for the sometimes wild or erratic amplitudes of an interior life.

Was I just lucky, or was there a fit in the world, waiting here for me already — waiting always — or is the answer somewhere in between?

Either consideration presumes a significance in the universe that probably does not exist. Most days I think the challenge is not to parse out which of the two answers is most accurate, but to simply remember to be grateful that it is so, and to marvel at this ice-made blue valley. To take one step out into it, and then another, and another: as if stepping out into the fabric of time itself. It is not so much like I have finally found myself, after all these years, wandering into this corner of the West, as instead like I have gotten lost: lost in the best sense, so that I now belong to this landscape and can start over, can be made anew. Can be shown new things, can make mistakes, can even fail.

And can then succeed.

I have two goals in this book: to examine how a place can change a person, and to explore why it's worth fighting to protect — for its own sake, as well as our own, all of us. I think our work in the Yaak is becoming a primer in true grass-roots work on the front lines, or, to use the terminology of the times, conservation work in the war zone. I think in this regard it is of universal value, even if someone doesn't care, or thinks he or she doesn't care, about a specific place called the Yaak itself.

1

Why I Came West

THE FORCES OF NATURE are huge, and we are tiny, and in the mountains it's easier to remember this. I don't think we'll ever figure out for sure if the details of our lives, or even the patterns of them, are the result of intricate, foreordained design or simply the exquisitely random windblown flutterings of grace and confusion.

I live in, or rather below, the mountains for two basic reasons: because I think mountains are one of the last huge and wild and magnificent things we have left in this country, one of the last few things we have not yet, in places, grasped and squeezed and sculpted into some unrecognizable, and diminished, shape — a landscape, therefore, in which possibility still exists; and because in 1975 or thereabouts, Robert Redford starred in a movie called *Jeremiah Johnson,* which was filmed in Utah, in some of the most beautiful country I had ever seen.

We all remember critical moments in our lives when the

senses were so deeply, and newly, touched — by a poem, a teacher, a book, a camping trip — and for me, that movie was one of those events. Sometimes I forget about Utah, and often I forget about art, about the aesthetic value of conjoining structure with idea and emotion, as that movie did.

I don't remember if I saw the movie in a theater or on television. I might have watched it on Mars, so captivated was I by the visuals and — as a young man, an adolescent, really — by the story, a man running away to a new beginning, and recovery. I remember the physical senses — Johnson thrashing around in snow and cold water, chasing a trout; Johnson by a smoking campfire; Johnson being solitary, and struggling with that solitude, some days despairing, others exultant — and thinking, as a young man, *I know this person.* I remember after the movie was over watching to see where it had been filmed: the strange names of those mountains and the national forests. I went to an atlas that evening and looked them up on the map. I found the nearest college towns to those forests: Logan, Ogden, Salt Lake, Provo . . . I wanted to study wildlife science, in the mountains, in the West.

Because of the mountains in that movie, I went to Logan, to Utah State University, where they put me on the fourth floor of a seven-story dorm in what was known as the Gentile sandwich: three floors of Mormons above and three below, with the thin supply of out-of-state students — pot-smoking ski bums, most of them — packed into the fourth floor. Surrounded. And metamorphosed, as if by landscape, yes.

I don't intend here to make cheap and easy fun of a culture, a religion, of such significant integrity, one with so many admirable values. I only want to say that being isolated, an alien in a strange and beautiful landscape in which it sometimes seemed I had as much in common with the rivers and stones and deer as with the people, was another of my lucky breaks. The world has become quickly small, and whatever we can do to make it seem large again, even if only in a few places, is probably a good thing.

I'd been around a Mormon or two before — I was aware of certain things about them, such as how they'd say, "Oh my heck," or "H-E-double toothpicks" instead of *hell* — but by and large Utah State was an immensely new cultural territory for me: a new culture to go with a new landscape.

Did I want to become a mountain man like Jeremiah Johnson? Probably, yes. On weekends I'd haul off across the tops of the mountains on snowshoes with no tent, only a down sleeping bag, no matter what the temperature or weather. I'd make little lean-tos, build little fires, and read books all weekend long, shivering, turning the pages with clumsy mittened hands. Glad to be out of Houston. Glad to have a vision, even if only, for the time being, a borrowed one, from someone else's work and art.

Scanning the course catalogue for easy but interesting electives, I chose by whim and whim alone a couple of bookish classes — an appreciation of the short story taught by Moyle Rice, and an essay writing class by Tom Lyon. I had no intention of ever becoming a writer, and had no idea, no way of knowing, that I had fallen into the pie and had signed on with the two finest writing instructors I would ever know. It was all chance and luck. But I suspect I would never have become a writer without those two classes, at the right time, in the right place. (I was not a natural scholar, and neither did I bring any significant amount of previous book learning with me. When, in the short story class, Moyle Rice was rhapsodizing about the work of a certain writer by the name of Flaubert, I spent twelve weeks believing he was referring perhaps to a great Native American chief of the region: Flow-Bear. I assumed then, and still do, that all literature is regional.)

In the spring I'd head south to the red rock country to smell the sage and track poisonous Gila monsters — an endangered species — through the sand, following their singular swag-bellied trails through the heated dunes. I continue to suspect that growing up in the suburbs of Houston as I did was only one of the greatest determining factors in developing a love and a need for wild country. Thank God there is still some of it left, even if it's not all protected yet. (Though even there, in Houston, my memories are strangely not of its awfulness but of nature: of hearing, for the first time each year, the autumn cry of migrating geese, and tasting — above the perpetual tang of benzene — the first cold front, or what passed for a cold front down there in the tropics. The strange prehistoric architecture of crawdads, latticed light falling through the longleaf pines, skinks rattling in dry oak leaves, locusts shrilling in summer. My childhood memories of Houston, from the very beginning, might as well be as those from a great and deep wilderness.)

By examining my deeper memory — that which I am able to extract or which resurrects itself whenever I return to visit Houston — I can see those things about Houston, the petrochemical horrors, that surely must have existed then but that simply, against the seeming odds, failed to attach to me or the developing template of who-I-would-become and what-I-would-love. How could I have ignored, or never noticed in the first place, the clotted tangle of skyline billboards, the 99 percent soil saturation by concrete, the perpetual clanking, tangled glitter-and-chrome gnarl of gridlocked traffic? The hissings and belchings of smokestacks elicited from me back then no more angst than had they appeared in a distant harmless dreamscape. Where was I, really, in those years, present-but-not-present, as if existing instead in some West-dormant waiting-upon period?

There in Houston, as a child, I would from time to time hear whisperings and rumors of the farther West; and despite the condition of that highly urbanized and then suburbanized city, I still somehow came to believe in an ethos of the West, however that might be defined. Indeed, not so terribly long ago, part of Texas might have been included in that ethos, just as another part of it would have been included in that of the Deep South.

Whatever the West was, however — and in my mind it was wild country, with a healthy population of wild and free creatures, their comings and goings, their habits and processes largely unhampered and uninhibited by the interference or prejudices of mankind — I sensed that it lay just a little farther on, a bit beyond the reaches of Houston.

The West has perhaps always been this way — it just keeps moving — and when I was a child growing up on the outskirts of Houston I believed that I had just missed it, the West, by only a single generation, or at the most two, as maybe every generation believes it has just missed the West. Perhaps not just heat-washed clodhopper farm boys standing discontented hoe-side in gypsum-strangled Utah, or wildcatters dreaming fevered uranium dreams or visions of oil-laden anticlines like sugarplums, but maybe residents of all centuries have stood on a mesa and wondered at a farther, deeper wildness — over the next range of mountains, if not also further back in time. And even then, might they have understood or intuited that their place in that time, believed to be enduring, would in fact prove to be far more prone to disintegration than the physical elements of mountains, forest, plains?

A hundred and forty years ago, Major John Wesley Powell, the one-armed Civil War veteran who explored the Grand Canyon and much of the rest of the West, said the unifying thread of the West was water, or the absence of it, and for sure that was, and largely is, one of the major physical threads. But there is something else too, some unseen thread of spirit. Perhaps it's best not to pick or pluck at that thread too closely — perhaps what we perceive as spirit in the West is really only something as heartless and lifeless as geology, with the rock outcroppings of the East being some several million years older, so that the half-life decay of sun-burnished ions in the West seems still to radiate a bracing and at times intoxicating freshness, able still to be felt and noticed if not yet measured by even a species as insensate and oblivious as our own. Perhaps science will one day ultimately be found to be at the heart of religion, or faith — as almost everything, it seems, is eventually discovered or named or measured or otherwise colonized — but for now, no such explanation or discovery exists, only the inexplicable awareness that there is a difference between the West and the rest of the country, and that it is no less profound for its ungraspable immeasurability.

So powerful can be this bond between westerners and landscape that it's possible to believe that the West might have existed in our brainpans long before the first paleface ever dreamed of conquest, possession, and that shadowed and seemingly illogical and inconsistent paradox, freedom. As human culture in the Deep South and the East is stacked in vertical layers of time, like geological strata, perhaps the building blocks of the West, particularly today's West, the New West, are composed of chunks of physical space — basin and range, sunlight, boulder, forest, river, desert — possessing more of a horizontal breadth.

To say the West was always in motion would be conjecture. What can be said confidently is that it is moving now — moving with such alacrity, like an animal getting up from a resting place and traveling for a while, that almost anyone can see it, and that even in those places where we cannot see it we can sense its movement, its possible going away or leave-taking, and we are made uneasy by it, even as we are still, at this late date, yet unable to name or measure that going-awayness, that freshness and wildness, that westernness.

Certainly in 1960s Texas it, the West, was going away like a horrific backwash. Each Sunday on our way to church my family would pass the informally named Wolf Corner, where I would lean forward in my seat to see the corner fence post where ranchers had hung that week's bounty, the little coyotes and the larger red wolves, by their heels, for all the honest world to see. It was out by Highway 6, which was once gently waving grassland — it's blanketed now with dazzling superstores, a twelve-lane highway, and vertical glittering skyscrapers reflecting the hot Houston sun in myriad directions, like the light envisioned perhaps by the prophets who beheld in their own exalted dreams the streets of heaven (assuming they were not holding the wrong end of the spyglass and witnessing instead the oppositional alternative territory described by those same prophecies). But back then it was only sweet balming tall-grass prairie, which yielded weekly its grisly bounty — the little wolves' legs fractured and bloodstained from where they had gnawed for hours or even days at the traps' grip, some of the wolves and coyotes stiffened and sun-dried, hanging like loose shingles after a storm, and others, newly killed, still limp and soft, like sheaves of tobacco hanging in some deathly curing house.

Always there was something there, placed partly as warning and partly as triumphant victory-show, a marker of how the war — against . . . what? obsolescence, frailty, insignificance, loss? — was faring. Some weeks there were more carcasses than others, and over the years the offerings gradually declined, though almost always there would be at least one, as if the ranchers were trawling the grassy sea, and as if their nets would always find something, some wildness deep within that green grass. As if that country to the west — just beyond the barbed-wire corner fence post — would slow but never entirely cease in giving the wolves up.

This was the dailiness and drama of my childhood, situated peculiarly between the Deep South and the far West, in oil-hungry, oil-rich, brash and arrogant and violence-born Anglo Texas. The vertical currency — the strata of time — mattered, but the story, the myth, of the West's frontier was also present, just over the horizon, and just beyond the field from which those wolves and coyotes had been gleaned. There was not just the echo of it; there was still, barely, the real and physical essence of it — we saw it, every Sunday. In those first few years of the 1960s, while the rest of the country — the Southeast, the Northeast, and Los Angeles in particular — stewed and boiled over civil rights issues, we were attending the premieres of movies such as *How the West Was Won* (1962) and *The Alamo* (1960), in which — not to sound too much like a bleeding-heart liberal — vast territory existed for the taking and, quite naturally, force was the way to take it, particularly since it was inhabited by Mexicans or Indians. Let Mississippi stew over drinking fountains and bus seats, and Boston and New York argue over segregated schools and busing; in Texas, we were busy looking longingly to the past, and to the West.

So with this background maybe I was always secretly summoned to this far corner of Montana, but a movie — art — helped fuel me. And in Utah, as a student, whenever I'd haul off into the Wellsville Mountains and scramble across the slatey talus slopes, examining the fossils of trilobites from half a billion years ago — when I'd splash out into the Bear River marsh, chasing giant carp, or when I'd hunt wild pheasants in the cattails — I would be aware, even as a young man, that all of that bounty came basically from the genesis of having sighted, and been touched by, the view of those same mountains in a film.

Maybe I should stop overstating the obvious; maybe in our olden lives — once upon a time, thousands of years ago — grace and bounty did not seem miraculous but were instead commonplace. But how rare, and how treasured, bounty seems, these days: bounty of any kind. And every time I look at these mountains where I live now, I remember debts: an awkward enough word, which surely does not exist in the relationship between mountains and mankind but which is as close as I can come to describing the imbalance between what I think the mountains give us and what we give back.

In Utah, playtime ended; I finished school and had to go to work. Witnessing the unhappiness of several friends in the field of wildlife management — prisoners of paperwork — I had changed my major to geology. (I hadn't yet even dreamed, at that point, of becoming a writer.) I took a job in Mississippi — was sucked back east, as if the world does not desire for our old cut grooves to be jumped so easily —

where, as a geologist, making maps of the invisible worlds below, I tracked the unanswerable comings and goings of ancient, buried oceans, imagining landscapes below as sublime as those here above in the present.

It was a fantastic life, that first one, the life of a geologist; or rather, perhaps it was already my second life, with childhood and its mystery-filled passage the true first. Then in this second life, the mapper, the oil cartographer, the dreamer, was given only the smallest clues, the smallest data points hinting at any possible solution to the mystery, with even those known facts few in number: a certain lithology found at one known depth or another, and a known porosity at one tiny sample point, gotten from a single borehole sunk into that old underground sea, frozen now in a tractless expanse of stone — a wilderness of stone.

The eight-and-five-eighths-inch drill hole letting such a tiny shaft of light, or space, back into that tight-locked heart of rock, rock that had not known the light of the sun in more than a hundred million years that such brief and limited awareness to the mapper was really no more tangible than the sudden pulses, the spears and shafts of light, that infiltrate one's vision sometimes when one turns to look for a bird, alerted to its passage not by the bird itself but by a quick-drifting shadow. And in so whirling, the mapper sees not the bird but only the blazing sun.

And yet armed with but a handful of such piercings, such dream fragments, the geologist proceeds, and sometimes he or she is successful.

How much of such success, then, is science, and how much

luck, and how much faith? What is the role of desire and passion in such pursuits? I believe that of the latter, much was, and is, required; and that in the pursuit, even more is generated. Eventually, however, the passion can wear down, wind down, run out. What tempered balance is finally struck, in one's life and in one's labors — and should one ultimately accept the nearing of that balance or instead continue to howl at the ever-present injustice?

Certainly, there was no winding down for me, back then: all the world was so new, and so much was possible. I was in Mississippi for a while: but that first, fierce vision of Utah's mountain landscape was held within me, as were held the countless subsequent visions, memories, and images of physical engagement that followed from that initial heart's response.

If landscape is direction for some of us, what will we do when it is lost — or rather, when the grand and the sublime within it are lost?

I think I knew all along, while I was in Mississippi — and I was there for eight years — that it was not the right fit. Possessing the malleability as well as vigor of youth, however, I made out all right; I engaged with the world, fed my senses, and glided. In retrospect, I was gliding toward Montana, though I would never have realized it then, holed up in the hardwood forests and riding my bike through the green pastoral landscapes of agriculture. Nor would I have realized my eventual arc or summons — not even a clue of it, or a yearning — while working as a geologist, probing those old landscapes that were nearly three hundred million years old, and sniffing around like a bloodhound for old oil, the sweet black distillation that no one had ever seen before, had never touched or smelled or burned before. Searching, with hunger, even if for the wrong thing.

Or rather, for me, at that time, it was the right thing. Later on — and these days, I am amazed I lasted eight years — it would become the wrong thing, and I would have to start over and go out and find the right thing, which would be a valley I had never even known existed, had never even heard of.

But for a while there in Mississippi, strange as it may seem, it might have been the right thing for me at the right time, even if it wasn't the place or time that was meant for me, or, certainly, me for it.

Is not love also this same way?

After a few years in Mississippi, it was revealed to me that I was not really executive or even office material. I took my leave from that job — if I recall correctly, I quit in a pique of temper, though it now seems so long ago that perhaps my departure was more graceful than I recall — and I began working as a consultant out of my little farmhouse.

My girlfriend, Elizabeth, was an artist, a painter and illustrator, and our days were pretty halcyon; in that regard, it was the perfect place and time for me. I'd started writing, and so each morning I would go out into the field before it got too hot and sit shirtless at an old white metal table and work there until the sun grew too hot and the overhead light too brilliant, at which point I'd go back inside the shady farmhouse and draw maps of buried treasure.

Later in the afternoon, I'd go over to Elizabeth's farmhouse, between Vicksburg and Natchez, on the Big Black Bayou. We'd go for a bike ride, or hang out in the hammock.

Closer to dusk, we'd go into town and play tennis, then go out to dinner and a movie, or would wander the grounds of the old Vicksburg Battlefield National Park. Then we'd go back to her farmhouse, and the next day, the world, and our youth, would open up all over again, with pretty much the same wonderful pacing, though with enough slightly different variations each day — new things explored, or old favorites revisited — to keep us in love with that world and, not least of all, each other. The days were like the fine beds of strata that form in perfect parallel, one thin day atop another, as if at the bottom of a still lake, and then one year after another.

And then things changed, for no reason I can yet plumb or fathom. Not between us and each other but between us and that place, and us and that time.

Blind to consequence but knowing all that we needed to know — knowing the direction of our hearts — we got up and left our sleepy lives in Mississippi and headed west again: not quite desperate but suddenly awakened is how I guess I'd have to describe it. We loaded an old pickup and drove north and west, casting north then west, searching for a place that could match inside the strength of that first view that had taken root and then grown.

When we left Mississippi, we desired a place with forests, meadows, rivers, mountains of course, solitude, proximity to vast public wildlands, and free rent. We wanted a place where I could write and Elizabeth could paint.

We started out looking in New Mexico, didn't find it — looked in Utah, almost found it — then headed up into Idaho and Montana before wandering across a summit and looking down onto a small green valley with a winding little river carving through it and smoke rising from a few chimneys, even though it was August, cool, blue August. We had no way of knowing then that the initial homestead we looked down upon from that summit where we first fell in love with yet another new landscape was the home of Mr. and Mrs. McIntire, whose son Tim had written the music for a movie called *Jeremiah Johnson*.

It was ten miles to the next homestead, the next little cabin with smoke rising blue. We drove on through an emotionally exhausting mix of magical old forests and clearcuts, old larch forests then clearcuts. We drove on down into the center of the valley, where — on that same first day — we found an abandoned lodge whose owners needed someone to live in it — for free — and we told them that we would.

I forget about my great good luck of making it as far north as Utah, straight out of high school, before being bounced back, pinball-like, to Mississippi for a while. And sometimes — enmeshed in such a physical world — I forget about the great good luck of art — seeing a certain movie at a certain time, or about lessons and ideas from those writing classes taught by Tom Lyon and Moyle Rice: the notion that art is selectivity. The urge to reassemble that which is loose and disparate, or, increasingly, that which is unraveling: this is the artist's sensibility, and the artist's response to life.

Are we drawn to certain places, and certain other lives, or does the world squeeze and shape and sculpt and direct us — often via our predisposition toward those places, and those lives?

I do not think it is a question that either scientists or artists will be able to answer. I think some things — some answers — are meant to remain a mystery, and might even possess shifting answers, with one aspect being true on one day and another the next. As even the seasons — despite their connections to one another — are always shifting, always living, and moving.

2

Landscape and Imagination

I SENSE SOMETIMES I SHOULD stop chasing this question, if only for my peace of mind, but it remains for me so utterly elusively a fundamental question: whether a person is shaped most by the iron rails of blood lineage or by the land and the strong and supple hands of experience. Perhaps one reason that the question matters to me so much is that regardless of the answer, the implication is clear: wild, unique landscapes, with their ability to provide powerful and unique experiences, are then in either case hugely valuable to us — possessing, surely, a value far in excess of our ability to measure or otherwise quantify or evaluate.

I had never considered such things until I moved to a dark wooded valley of hermits tucked tight against the border of Montana and Canada, but I have been considering these questions since, while marveling at what I perceive to be landscape's phenomenal sculpting ability upon the lives and emotions of not just children but grown men and women, for whom the die of character and destiny presumably has already been cast.

I've seen it happen both ways: men and women arriving here who are almost a ready-made fit for this dark, cold, rainy, secretive, moody place, and men and women arriving too who have had none of these attributes, who were instead cheerful, bright, outgoing, even ebullient, but who quickly became — over the course of only a full year's cycle — withdrawn, pensive, paranoid, erratic.

One often hears about how an artist sculpts or shapes his or her work and how, sometimes, the artist's work then helps shape or direct culture. It seems to me that we hear less often how the artist's subject sculpts the artist. Speaking only for myself, I can't help but be struck by the notion that despite this artist-subject relationship, sometimes there is also something standing behind me as I work, watching me watch the subject, and that perhaps that secret observer is some elusive, unknowable shadow of the subject. What is essential, wrote Saint-Exupéry, is invisible to the eye. What is the name of this thing, this shadow, this core of art? Is it — this unseen essence — not also present, indisputably present, when one walks through the cathedral of an ancient forest or along the windy spine of some high mountain ridge?

Surely these invisible cores of mystery are one of the great sources of story, of art, of emotion. You can look at a painting of sunlight on a bowl of fruit and feel a yearning in your heart, some emotion, some deep sense of sorrow or joy or pleasure, that has nothing whatsoever to do with fruit. Quite often this emotion was possibly the thing passing from behind the artist, watching the artist watch and paint that fruit; passing through the artist's heart, perhaps, like an arrow, and then into the fruit.

Or perhaps that penetrating gaze comes from the subject, the fruit, and passes right through the artist and into the mysterious place residing just behind the artist; I don't know.

All I mean to be suggesting is that in landscape we often sense and know vibrantly, dramatically, that what is essential is indeed invisible to the eye, and that in wilderness perhaps above all other places this phenomenon can be most keenly known and felt.

In speaking of this shadow or watcher or place behind or just beyond the artist, I'm not talking about the Muse, which I think of as inspiration — the fuel or force that makes you get up and go to work in the morning. What I'm wondering about is something else, some third, mysterious thing, between us and the imagination, between our landscape (internal or external) and our imagination.

I hesitate to use the word, but use it I must: *spirit.* The spirit that exists not in us, and not upon the land, but between us and the land, like an electrical current generated. I believe this spirit, this ribbon between things, is generated when a certain individual or a certain species enters a certain landscape — just as when, in a story, a certain character enters the landscape of that story. You can't measure or quantify or even see such a thing, but anyone can feel it.

Speaking only for myself, I feel some days that a balance is being lost between me and this other thing that is created or set in motion when I enter a landscape. For me, personally, of late, I've lost much of my heart and the spark or fire that once "created," or produced, the art of fiction. So dominant is the landscape into which I've moved that it seems almost always that the shadow of this place is behind me, watching — sometimes with interest, other times with boredom, but almost always watching — whatever it is I'm up to on the page.

I think to some degree this overawareness is because I've come gradually, in every sense of the word, to be a resident of the Yaak — not just physically, but spiritually. This land and its people enter my dreams. I stare at the same woods each day, sunrise and sunset. I hear the same passing ravens, see the same deer and bears; I am as entwined in the rhythm of the weather and seasons as any of the other plants or animals. I have become a part of my subject, enmeshed in it. I am no longer on the outside of it, an alien observer.

Too much of this awareness can at times become a hindrance to art. It is taking me some effort to get used to my awareness of this shadow. Some days it's like trying to write while a strange hawk or eagle is perched on my shoulder. I feel often that I am in some sort of transition as an artist because of this. I do not know whether to try to shoo the observer, the awareness, away, or become accustomed to and comfortable with it and move in even closer.

I've been trying to write seriously for over twenty years now. I think if I were going to have it figured out — how to separate the artist from the human being, or the artist from the subject, or the artist from the landscape. I would have done so by now. What I think is that most of the time it is a big tangled mess. A mystery, and a shifting blend. Maybe I shouldn't even be talking about it.

Certainly, how my wife and I got to this blue valley is a mystery, one that I've only recently come to accept as having been inevitable. Back in Mississippi, when that strange and sudden feeling of restlessness came over us, we just got in the truck and drove, and left Mississippi. I had been writing short stories for a couple of years down there, but as a writer, I had begun to panic: it seemed suddenly to me that the same two colors, green and yellow, were repeating themselves in story after story, as were my characters and their mannerisms. As well, I missed the mountains of northern Utah and was homesick for that spaciousness. Time is the great terrain of the South, in the landscape of history — but the landscape of the West was new to me, seeming infinite, and horizontal rather than vertical.

What did I know? Nothing: only that I missed the West's terrain of space. Elizabeth and I vaulted west, young and strong and healthy, and not, coincidentally, new-in-love, and hit that huge and rugged landscape full in stride.

We drove north through the dense blue woods until we ran out of country — until the road ended and we reached the U.S.-Canada border — and then, rather than crossing over (for there was no crossing), we turned west and traveled until we almost ran out of mountains: to the back side of the Rockies, to the wet, west-slope rainforest.

We came over a little mountain pass — it was August by this time, and winter was already fast approaching, unseen but strongly felt — and looked down on the soft hills, the dense purples of the spruce and fir forests, and the ivory crests of the ice-capped peaks, and at the slender ribbons of gray thread rising from the chimneys of the few cabins nudged close to the winding river below, and we fell in love with that landscape, as they say, at first sight: falling the way people in movies fall with each other, star and starlet, as if a trapdoor has been pulled out from beneath them, tumbling through the air, arms windmilling furiously, and suddenly no other world but each other, no other world but this one, and eyes for no one, or no place, else . . .

What I thought first about that beloved supple landscape, with its velvet folds and curves, was that it was one pure thing, distilled. How else could it, as well as its moods and rhythms, be so deeply felt as unique even to us, pilgrims, immediately upon our arrival? But what I came to learn gradually was that the valley's identity comprised not an irreducible, elemental distillation but rather something more fragile and wonderful, more organic and complex: the fated meshing, always, of two things.

As if a person were to have two voices, or two identities, or two lives. There was twice the amount of richness, twice the amount of mystery. There was a suppleness in the landscape, because of these two things — the valley was caught in a magic seam between the snowy, stony austerity of the northern Rockies and the lush rainforest tropics of the Pacific

Northwest. Because of this duality — almost everywhere you looked, two things were always present instead of one: fire and char standing right next to fungal rot — there was a distinct and forceful narrative, not the vertical narrative of time, which so distinctly permeates the Deep South, but the horizontal, more western narrative of space, open space, much of it unexplored and unknown. In all physical things, I think, resides the easy and willing opportunity for metaphor.

And to any given duality — between any two given things or conditions — there cannot help but be a tension, whether great or small. The birth of narrative.

It is this space between things, and always, in this landscape, the ready presence of two ways of thinking rather than one, that stirs my imagination; and this landscape, this blue valley, continues to carve at me, as I try to find the right wedge or seam, the right rhythm and way of being, into which to settle.

I was a hunter before I came up here, but not to the degree I am now. It astounds me sometimes to step back, particularly at the end of autumn, and the end of hunting season, and take both mental and physical inventory of all that was hunted, and all that was gathered, from this newer, stranger, dreamier life in the mountains.

The woodshed groaning tight, full of firewood. The fruits and herbs and vegetables from the garden, canned and dried or frozen, and then also the wild fruits as well, the huckleberries, mountain thimbleberries, and wild strawberries, and the smoked trout and whitefish; the wild mushrooms; and most precious of all, the flesh of the wild things that share with us these mountains and the plains to the east — the bull elk, the whitetail and mule deer bucks; the ducks and geese, grouse and pheasant and Hungarian partridge and dove and chukar; the wild turkey. Each year, the cumulative bounty seems unbelievable. What heaven is this into which we've fallen?

Most days, such is your joy and wonder at being gifted with such a life that you feel as if there's nothing else you can do but write, or paint, or sing; it is not so much the wild meat and fruit you have eaten that compel you to feel this way as it is the simple curves and flexes of the earth, and your own gradual fit into these curves and bends. Again, the landscape — and the tension between you and it, as you come to know it — provides a stimulus for art, and a stimulus for the imagination, as you consider the nearness between any two certain things, or the distance between any two other things.

Always, in the great diversity of a wild landscape like the Yaak, there are two things. Nothing has been fully settled yet. There are two species of deer, two species of eagle. Two types of bears — black and grizzly. Two kinds of everything.

It's been said of art that a story is about but one thing: a man or woman wants something, and goes after it, and in the process wins, loses, or comes to a draw. What else is this also but a description of the hunt? One sets out after one's quarry with the senses fully engaged, wildly alert: entranced, nearly hypnotized. The tiniest of factors can possess the largest significance — the crack of a twig, the shift of a breeze, a single stray hair caught on a piece of bark, a freshly bent blade of grass.

What else is the hunt but story, or the pursuit of story, and always a stirring of the imagination, with the quarry or goal or treasure lying just around the next corner, or just over the next rise? I find it not coincidental that the rich, magical landscape of the Yaak — this dark forest — contains more different types of hunters — carnivores — than any valley in North America. It is a predator's showcase, home not just to wolf and grizzly but wolverine, lynx, bobcat, marten, fisher, black bear, mountain lion, golden eagle, bald eagle, coyote, fox, weasel . . . In the Yaak, everything eats meat and everything is in motion, either seeking its quarry or seeking to keep from becoming quarry.

You don't have to write a story about such goings-on, but such spirit gives you a certain support, I think, to know that all around you, you are up to your armpits in story: that you are supported by the culture of story.

Sometimes, on a good day, even when all you mean to be doing is resting, or going for a hike, or hunting, the pace of the landscape around you will pick you up, or will pick up your subconscious imagination and carry you with it; and if you didn't bring a piece of paper with you on your walk, you'll find yourself scribbling notes on a piece of birch bark, about some newly imagined or newly felt story, and if you didn't bring a pen, you'll be carving, with shorthand, the idea onto a branch, which you'll carry home with you that night for transcription. Because you are of the landscape, you try to keep up with it; you adjust yourself to its rhythms.

As an artist, I find it deeply important that such places, such wild places, be protected wherever they are still to be found.

The hunted shapes the hunter; the pursuits and evasions of predator and prey are but shadows of the same desire. The thrush wants to remain a thrush, the goshawk wants to consume the thrush — and in so doing, partially become the thrush: to take its flesh into its flesh. They weave through the tangled branches of the forest up here, zigging and zagging, the goshawk right on the thrush's tail, like a shadow. Or perhaps it is the thrush that is the shadow thrown by the light of the goshawk's fiery desire.

Either way, the escape maneuvers of the thrush help carve and shape and direct the muscles of the goshawk. This slight, slight distance between them — the dramatic tension — is story. Even when you are walking through the woods up here, seeing nothing but trees, you can feel the unseen passage of such stories that might have occurred earlier that morning, in the precise place where you are standing — pursuits that will doubtless, after you are gone, sweep right back across that same spot again and again.

Some landscapes these days have been reduced to nothing but dandelions and fire ants, knapweed and thistle, where the only remaining wildlife to be found are sparrows, squirrels, and starlings. In the blessed Yaak, however, it is all still present: not a single species has gone extinct since the retreat of the Ice Age. I find this astounding, and magical; I know of no other valley in the continental United States for which this can be said. The biota of the Yaak is the ecological equivalent of a Russian novel. It is a greatness, an ecological heritage, that we still have, barely, in the possession of public ownership. Unlike the Russian novels, however, which are preserved forever in libraries, the last roadless wildlands of the Yaak are not preserved: there is no guarantee of their continued survival, or of the survival of that wildness, that art, that exists between our imaginations and the landscape.

The eagles and lions, bears and wolves, owls and hawks, are not the only hunters in this northern landscape. This landscape summons — or shapes, and creates — human hunters. Almost anyone who has lived here for any period of time has ended up — sometimes almost as if against one's conscious wishes, and in the face of preexisting biases — becoming a hunter, to varying degrees.

This is a magnificent landscape, a wild and powerful landscape, and again, it sculpts us like clay. I do not find such sculpting an affront to or diminution of the human race and the human spirit, but rather, wonderful testimony to our pliability, and our ability, still, to be accepted into the place of things.

I'm convinced there is a third spirit. The spirit within us, and the spirit of a place, and then that third thing, that story-like thing — the ignition, or spark, that occurs between us and it. The braid of those two things flowing, like some river.

There is no guarantee, no certainty, of this thing's survival. It is a gift, a blessing.

I myself love, love, to hunt the deer, the elk, and the grouse, to follow them into the mouth of the forest, to disappear in their pursuit — to get lost following their snowy tracks up one mountain and down the next — and each year during such pursuits, I am struck more and more by the conceit that people in a hunter-gatherer culture might occasionally have access to richer imaginations than those who dwell more fully in an agricultural or even post-agricultural environment.

Here is how it might work. A hunter's imagination might have no other choice but to become more deeply engaged, when entering into the hunt, for it is never the hunter who is in control but rather, always, the hunted, in that the prey directs the predator's movements.

The hunters imagine where the deer might be, or where it might go. They follow the tracks laid down like clues — tracks speaking not only to distance and direction traveled but also pace and gait and the general state of mind of the animal that is evading them. They plead to the mountain to deliver to them a deer, an elk. They imagine, and hope that they are moving toward, the unknown. How can such movement be anything but art, and story?

However, in a non-hunting society — an agricultural society, for instance (though perhaps I oversimplify here) — when you plant a row of corn, there is not so much unknown. You can be fairly sure that if the rains come, the corn is going to sprout, that that corn is not going anywhere, is not seeking to elude you.

But when you step into the woods, looking for a deer — well, there's nothing in your mind, or in your blood, or in the world, but imagination.

To simplify it further: in the post-agricultural society, too often we confuse anticipation with imagination.

When we wander down the aisle of the supermarket, searching for a fecal sludge chunk of chicken, or when we cruise into the department store, searching for that one sweater, or almost any sweater, we can be fairly confident that, thanks to the vigor and efficiency of a supply-and-demand marketplace, that grayish wad of chicken or that sweater is going to be there. The imagination never quite hits second gear.

Does the imagination atrophy from such chronic inactivity? I don't know. I suspect that it does.

This is only what works for me — I would hope never to be so blind as to offer it as prescription. I offer it only as testimony to my love of the landscape where I live — a place that is still, against all odds, its own place, quite unlike any other place — but I do not think that I personally would be able to sustain myself as a writer if I did not take off three months of each year to wander the mountains in search of game: to hunt as if stretching or exercising not just my imagination but my spirit. And to wander the mountains too, in all the other seasons. And to be somehow nourished by that third thing, that river of spirit that flows, shifting and winding, between me and the land.

Imagination can be two things: making a new and better fit, or escaping, carving one's way out of an awkward or ill fit and stepping into a space or time of new possibilities.

For those of us living in this blue valley, our old stories are that we came here under the latter premise, imagining and hoping for a better way, and our new stories are that many of us are engaged daily in a struggle to make the new fit — sometimes laboring to shape our lives in a certain manner, though other times finding that we are achieving the newer fit almost effortlessly, seamlessly; that through dreams and the imagination, we are being carried along on the momentum of some greater force, the immense force of time, usually, though in such a vast landscape as this one, perhaps we are carried also by the sheer momentum of all the physical space looming above and around our own puniness.

To put this notion of fit, of sculpting, more succinctly, the late John Gardner and others have said that there are only two stories in the world: a man or woman goes on a journey, or a stranger rides into town.

Either way, the story is again a question of fit, and of being shaped — going on a journey to escape the old ill fit, or riding into town and seeking to discover or establish one's own new fit.

This landscape of the Yaak, the wild Yaak, carves the peaceable, and it carves the unpeaceable. Often finding myself at odds with those individuals possessing a large dose of the latter, I try, like a knee-jerk, bleeding-heart liberal, to consider their position: to try to deduce the source of their fierce belief in the dogma of complete control over the dreaded, mysterious wilderness.

The West has never been anything but a colony of the extractive industries, feasting (with the benefit of full congressional subsidy) on the splendor of these public wildlands. But the extractive industries have been very sly in doing everything they can to promulgate this myth of the rugged and completely independent individual: enhancing the already existing wall that stands between the rural West and the rest of the outside world; goading these little kings, each of us a little king, into believing these myths, right on up until the time that this or that multinational corporation — Champion International, Plum Creek Limited Partnership, Asarco, Pegasus Gold, Louisiana-Pacific, Georgia-Pacific, Noranda, or whomever — pulls the rug out from under our feet, having mined the last of the ore (leaving us, and the taxpayers, with the cleanup) or having cut the last of the big timber (leaving us, and the taxpayers, with the subsequent challenges of reclamation) — having found cheaper labor, cheaper transport, cheaper or more plentiful resources, elsewhere — and leaving town, sometimes bothering to name a scapegoat on the way out (always environmentalists, never labor-saving technology or shareholder demands for greater quarterly profits), though other times simply leaving town without a word. Never, ever assuming responsibility. Possessing the rights of individuals, but in the end, unaccountable, vaporous, ungraspable.

As a sense of time's passage influences a southerner's art and personal landscapes, how can the physical landscape not influence a westerner's, or that of any other artist residing in a place that still has some physical uniqueness, some otherness — some thing-ness, as opposed to too much shadow-ness? In a wild or natural or unique place, landscape is setting, landscape is mood; certainly, landscape can be structure, and landscape as well can be a character — perhaps even the dominant character.

In the West, maybe it is this simple: William Shakespeare is rumored to have said that all literature is about loss or the recognition of loss. A westerner in the twenty-first century — or any inhabitant of wild country — lives immersed hourly in loss. How can art — an art that bears testimony to this truth — not emerge?

But have I boxed myself into a corner, speaking as an artist in praise of wild landscapes, of the need for the preservation, at least, of the last few little wild islands and gardens we have left in the otherwise much-raided treasury of the public lands? If the further trashing of these wild gardens produces further flux and loss, yielding in turn even more and perhaps finer, more heartfelt art, cannot it be said that something good occurs from such squandering? Something perhaps not as immortal as a mountain range or even as lasting as a river or a forest, but something perhaps more accessible, to a greater number of people these days — art?

I don't think so. I think we all sense that a compression, a strange diminishment, of both time and space is in full gallop now; if anything, perhaps a slowing down of the rate of loss of one or the other would be the abrupt thing, the flux, needed now to give a new pulse, another surge or jump start, to the artistic impulses. In any event, the world — both man's world and the natural world, or God's world — will change soon enough, with or without our efforts. We need vitally these last untouched, unmanipulated cores of wilderness, not just for their own beautiful sake, but to act as reference points against which we can gauge and perceive the distance between that world and this one.

It is across that distance, across that difference in space and time, that a certain type of art can continue to be created, across that distance and difference that a certain kind of narrative — sinuous, dramatic, and immense — can still flow, like electricity.

The world will never and should never become all one thing. There will always be some differences, enough differences, between which and in which artists will be able to continue to make art.

But the more similar our world and our culture becomes, the more we need wilderness. The more we become different from the wilderness, the more we need the wilderness. I myself need it, in the words of Ellen Burns Sherman from almost a hundred years ago, because I too believe that "the more civilized man becomes, the more he needs and craves a vast background of wildness . . . to which he may return, a contrite prodigal from the tasks of an artificial life."

People living in the city need it, if for no other reason than to keep from becoming like me, and I need it, if for no reason but to keep from becoming like them; for surely our different personalities and characteristics help strengthen and diversify us as a disparate yet collective nation. Surely this is one of the foundations upon which a vital democracy was formed: the ability to have choices. And I choose what little wild country is still left: that which might still nurture me and my kind.

I need a lot of that "vast background of wildness." Especially in the Yaak. I need all of the tiny, tiny amount that is left.

If it's small, it's not wilderness. If there becomes any less of it, it becomes less wild. The story of our dwindling wilderness has as its protagonist the essence of space, with the voracious character of time gnawing hungrily at its edges. The narrative is in full crisis, full climax, now.

I can still, however, imagine — barely — a happy ending.

3

Meat

SOMETIMES, FOR A LIVING, I will have to go out to the other side of the country — not the other side of the valley or the state, but the United States — and give a reading, a lecture, a workshop, regarding the ghost of one of my old lives, which was short story writing — the ghost I try always to keep near and hope soon to reinhabit.

And at those lectures, people who have known only pavement now for a very long time, sometimes their entire lives, will be confused when I try to describe my life to them — living off the grid and at the edge of a great unprotected wilderness, a life in which on any walk I am likely to see an owl, an elk, a bear, a lion, or at least the sign, the evidence, of these things — and then when I describe my life's goals, that we as a society need to commit to protecting the forests, the last wild mountains and rivers and creeks, the last high hanging hidden valleys, the last . . . everything — there is further confusion.

Every time, I see the uncertainty, the pure disappointment, come into their eyes as they do the math. *You want to protect those forests so you can keep going in there and . . . killing things,* they realize.

They're too polite to phrase it that way, and so instead they inquire, with slightly greater delicacy and tact, "How can you call yourself an environmentalist when you're a hunter?"

It is a question that has plagued all hunters for a long time, since before the modern conservation movement began — since hunters first initiated the conservation movement. It is hard to explain, hard to discuss — this choice, this summons, this identity, this way of being — without sounding defensive. Philosophers have discussed hunting for as long as there have been philosophers. The arguments of pesticide-soaked soybeans versus cattle versus wild elk are wearisome to me. I am not out to convert anyone to hunting. My concerns are about the ethics and manners and respect afforded the privilege (and necessity) of obtaining one's food from the land — from the world — in case anyone has forgotten that nothing, and no one, lives forever, and everything we do has a cost.

But I sometimes think that if a person who had doubts about hunting was able to experience what I have, he or she might feel differently about judging hunters; might not have an answer to the paradox and turmoil of emotions that surround the physical act, but at least might better understand the power, allure, and — for some — necessity of hunting. To see the dog's passion as it trails an invisible river of scent, glancing back over his shoulder to be sure you are still with him, and then leaping a hedge — or to cut fresh tracks in new snow at first light, to slip in downwind behind a herd of elk in the high country, and to pursue one of the big bulls — spawned out, rutted out, soon to be wolf bait, or lion bait, or, like each of us, earth bait — embedded in that herd, and to seek to maneuver oneself into position (with forty pairs of eyes watching, forty pairs of ears listening, forty elk cautious to every scent they can process) for a clean shot that drops the animal you've chosen (*this is not shopping*) in an instant.

And to then, after giving thanks to the elk, to the mountain, to the world, to begin the days-on-end process of gutting and cleaning so large an animal, and packing out, from so far in the roadless backcountry — which is the country of elk — one quarter at a time, hundreds of pounds of wild meat, two or three days of all-day packing, down the steep slopes, trading one's remnant youth and vitality, on aging joints and waning muscles, for that wild meat, wild air, wild scent, wild life — and spending the better part of the next week, then, in the ritual of processing one's own meat: not hiring out that responsibility to a stranger but continuing to care for — to steward — that which you have been fortunate enough to receive, or to go out and get. Separating tendon, ligament, and fascia from each deep red muscle — learning every strand of every muscle of that magnificent animal (there is no fat, none, in the muscles themselves; only red desire) and wrapping each choice cut, and labeling it, in preparation for the meals of the coming year.

It is a process, a continuum, a way of life, a relationship with the mountains, with the marshes, with the entire valley.

In the fall, it's what I want to do. It would be unnatural and dishonest to sit on my hands; I'm a hunter, a predator (in the fall), with eyes in the front of my head, like a bear's or a wolf's or even an owl's. Prey have their eyes on the sides of their heads in order to see in all directions, in order to be ready to run. But predators — and that's us, or at least some of us — have our eyes before us, out in front, with which to focus to a single point. For two months of the year — or until I have been fortunate enough to find and kill one deer and one elk — that's what I do. I want to be out in the woods, walking quietly, walking slowly — or not walking at all but just sitting in some leaves, completely hidden and motionless — waiting, and waiting. To not pursue the thing one wants would be a waste of one's life.

In the fall, I can do things I can't do in my normal, civilized life. I can disappear into the woods, and over the next mountain, the next ridge. My roaming has meaning — it's no longer just roaming, but hunting. The year's meat supply is in question. My meat, my family's meat — not some rancher's heifer from Minnesota. Meat from my valley, where I hope to live and die — where I cut firewood, where I pick huckleberries, where I walk, where I watch the stars — my valley.

I don't see it as paradox at all: I love to hunt. Not as much as I used to when I was a young man and could walk up and down the mountains all day, sometimes breaking into a trot simply because walking was too easy and did not match the burning inside me, and back when I could go to bed at the end of a long day and awaken at first light without a muscle's or joint's complaint and would be ready, and eager, to go again; but still I look forward to it each year, and still I enjoy it. The hunt more than any other season remains the fulcrum around which the rest of my year orbits.

For those two or three months, I am after something: something tangible, something that's moving away from me, and something that I must have for the coming year. It's as simple as that.

Over the next ridge. The new life of stores and towns falls away and the old life returns. There's a loveliness to looking ahead — looking straight ahead — that only hunting brings out.

The other ten months are okay too — I can be the artist. But the fall comes like a splash of water to my face on a hot, dusty day; and the dust, and my new ways, new feelings — the ones bound by rules — are washed away, leaving the old ways revealed.

I keep eating those lovely candlelit dinners — grouse and potatoes, and the red, almost *purple* hearththrob steaks from elk, fried trout for breakfast, and homemade huckleberry jam — and I feel alive. I draw immense strength from those meals, strength to live my life, and it feels good. When I was a younger man, I would eat about a pound and a half of this meat per day. The cancer studies for this kind of diet alarm me, but I have to trust that they apply to fatty steroid beef and cattle raised in pesticide fields. I was seven miles into the mountains when I shot last year's elk, and I carried him out in three trips over a twenty-four-hour period.

Into those same dark woods I go each year, looking straight ahead, and stopping, and listening, and turning my head.

Of course, it's possible that there's a greater force that judges us; and of course, sometimes I feel guilty about being a hunter, a killer — a killer of deer and elk, though not moose, because they're too easy, and not bears, because . . . well, bears themselves are meant to hunt. During part of the year they're predators, not prey. It seems unnatural to me to hunt predators.

I'm scared, sometimes, that all the animals I've killed — few as they are — add up, and that I'm liable for them.

I wouldn't mind paying with my life someday — we must all give up our lives — but sometimes I get scared that I may have to pay afterward, in the afterlife, for my gluttony, my insatiable hunger for clean meat, and so much of it.

Nonetheless, I've studied it and have come up with this: I am who I am, and I've come from the place we all come from — the past — but I still remember, and love, that place. Some of us are glad to be away from that place, but I'm not one of those people — not in the fall.

There may be different reasons for and ways of living a life, but certainly for me, those two criteria — engagement, and the passion of desire — are high on the list. They are in many ways the same paths that are followed in writing fiction, and in the imaginative mapping of unseen underground formations as a geologist.

There's nothing wrong with hunger, I think, or passion, or desire — on the contrary. It's gluttony, I think, that's the sin.

We each possess a cost, a physical weight, to remain in the world — an ecological footprint. But we each possess a moral footprint as well, and surely the cost, the price of admission, is remaining alert and engaged, attentive to and participating in this miraculous world and the miraculous, momentary condition of our lives, as opposed to just checking out, blanking out, and bumping along, gliding along, with such costs and issues unexamined, being disengaged. As if hiring out such passions, and our desires, to others.

The worst day I ever had hunting was when I shot an elk in the neck, but it made me feel bad after it was over. I broke the elk's neck, the way I always try to do — that instant drop — but he groaned when I walked up to him. He couldn't have been feeling anything, and I hope it was just air leaving his lungs as they deflated, but the sound it made was still that of a groan.

For a fact — or rather, for me — hunting's better than killing. It takes a while after it's over — sometimes a long while — before you can think of it as meat. You can't go straight from a living animal to 250 pounds of elk steaks. There's too much knife and ax work involved — and you're the one who has to do it — skinning the animal and pulling the hide back to reveal your crime, the meat, and already, sometimes, with the call of ravens drifting in, black-winged shapes flying through the treetops, past the sun.

Instead of trying to make that instantaneous conversion — which I cannot do — life to meat — what I do is pray, sort of. I give heartfelt, shaky thanks to the animal as I clean it, ravens calling to ravens, and I do this with deer and grouse too, and even, if I can remember — which I don't always —

with fish. A man or a woman who apologizes for hunting is a fool. It's a man's or a woman's choice, and he or she must live with it.

I watch ravens in the off-season. I think ravens understand the hunt better than I ever will. Sometimes ravens in Alaska lead hunters — wolves, or humans — to prey, and then they eat the pickings from the kill.

Ravens, black as coal, shiny and greasy, flying in the sun, like winged black devils . . . I feel as if I'm on their side, and it scares me, but it would be a lie, in the fall, to switch sides: to pretend that I'm not. I'm a killer sometimes. There are times when I wish I weren't, but I am. I've wrestled with it but can't escape it, any more than — until death — one can escape one's skin.

We are made of meat, not wood, and our eyes are in the front of our head. There is a spark that burns differently in some of us and I think it would be wrong, is wrong, for others to desire that the spark not be there. As long as we protect this same spark in the wild country itself, all these things should still remain sustainable, as eternal as the passing of geese in the night sky each autumn, or the turning of the leaves. To me, the two things — fighting tooth and nail to protect the last wild country in which this ancient and wilder spark still resides, and in the autumn going out into that country to look, with respect and gratitude, for game — are not incompatible but are in fact on the contrary inseparable.

4

The Question

FOR A FEW YEARS AFTER moving up here I would wake up wondering, almost every morning, whether I was taking the right course. I had quit my company job as an oil and gas geologist, was easing away from my job as a consultant, and had begun dabbling in fiction, only to get sucked, almost immediately, into activism: trying to help protect these wild places I was falling in love with. Had fallen in love with.

My transition from artistic pacifist to activist came pretty quickly, though certainly not all at once. When I arrived in this sylvan valley, warfare, strife, desperation, and the bitterness of steady defeat seemed — thank goodness! — the furthest thing from my mind. I was young and strong, and everything I saw — everything — was new and wonderful. I went for long walks through old dark forests and hiked to the tops of distant mountains, where I beheld beautiful views. Time seemed to me to be stopped cold in its tracks, for whenever I blinked, there was something new, something outlandish. My first sighting of a wolverine, first grizzly, first wolf. First princess pine, first kinnikinnick, first moose with summer velvet antlers, first marten, first harlequin duck, first bog orchid, first everything.

And, in the natural order of things, first summer, first autumn, winter, and spring.

It was around that second summer, as I recall, that my mind began to make comparisons, to notice what all was going on around me and the rate of that change: after I had experienced four full seasons, which provided me then with a reference point against the environmental practices — namely, the rampant clearcuts and plowing of dusty roads deep into the forest — that were proceeding.

That first year, I had noticed no harm, no fouls, because it had all been new, and as such frozen for me in time.

But it didn't take long. By the second year I had it figured out that those old clearcuts were still being made anew elsewhere around the valley, and it didn't take a rocket scientist to figure out there had to be a better way; nor did it take a genius to do the math and look at the valley, or even a map of the valley, and extrapolate the frenetic activity to a point at which the viewer understood — suddenly, it seemed — the arc of what was to come.

I eased into it, at first. There weren't a lot of local conservation efforts in the Yaak, per se — what little there was back then was focused more on the majestic rock-and-ice blade of the Cabinet Mountains, just to the south — but I began attending some of the meetings of the Cabinet-minded folks, and some of the Forest Service's public meetings too, particularly those that concerned the proposed management for grizzly bears, and mines, and issues relating to the wilderness, or the lack of it.

It was a pretty steep learning curve, and pretty rough country in which to be an environmentalist. The Champion mill was running at peak liquidation capacity, employing about 1,000 people (in a town of 2,400), and the mines were blowing and going too. That was about it for jobs: essentially a one-horse company town, subservient to the commodities markets. When the loggers and miners got in my face, I tended to jaw right back at them. I'd probably do it the same way all over again, but that's not how I do it now: or not as much, anyway. These days I'm far more interested in winning than in fighting. I sense deeply that the clock is running out.

Being a writer, I started to write about these issues in addition to attending meetings. It seemed inconceivable to me that such amazing country possessed no permanent protection whatsoever. Surely it was simply an oversight. And I thought that once I brought that oversight to the agency's, and Congress's, attention, there would be but a short time period before the correction and adjustment was made. It might take a year of pretty hard and focused work, I theorized, or maybe, given government's slowness, even a year and a half. I was more than willing to take that time off from my craft and devote it to the mountains and the valley. A full year seemed like a pretty long time, but so what? Brimming with energy, I had time on my hands, and — or so I believed

— time on my side. The fact that there had never been any wilderness designated in the Yaak simply meant to my opportunistic mind that the time had come.

There was so much change for me, back then, coming in so short a time. Was I right to be abandoning those new joys of fiction writing and the raw freedom of never knowing what each day would bring — never knowing the turns a story would take, and in fact following most stories in the direction opposite where I might ordinarily have expected them to wander — and to instead launch myself — carelessly, recklessly, wantonly, daily — into advocacy on behalf of the last roadless areas in a small wild valley? Back then I never dreamed that strength, energy, endurance, might someday be available in anything less than infinite supply.

It's the wildest and most diverse valley I've ever seen in the Lower Forty-eight, with grizzlies prowling around in the forests down to elevations as low as two thousand feet, as well as still possessing lynx, wolverines, wolves, sturgeon in the Kootenai River, great gray owls, bull trout, eagles, and on, and on . . . Still, despite this wildness, there is not one single acre of protected wilderness in the million-acre valley.

The question I used to ask myself — every morning — was a simple question, one to which — each morning — I had only to answer *yes* or *no*. Should I write about this valley in the real world, in real life, or should I continue on with my new joy, new profession, of fiction: made-up stories about make-believe lives in make-believe places?

Should I just keep quiet about the damage — the injustices — being done to the Yaak?

This ravaged valley, which has been clear cut to hell and back — only a tattered archipelago of roadless cores still remains intact — might be better off without my voice in almost every regard save that of my own conscience. The current human community of shy hermits and government-loathers that lives here might be more at ease were the plight of this valley's roadless lands still a secret, as might the present grizzly bear community (which at that point had dwindled rapidly to one remaining breeding-age female; now there are three) be better off, in the next few coming years, if I'd just lie low and be quiet. The old ways of road building and clear cutting are maybe, perhaps, just about gone, or surely soon to be gone, aren't they? (Though only ten and twenty years ago, they were not just about gone.)

It's true that the Yaak has been hacked hard, but maybe that's all over. Wasn't there a chance that without even having to say anything, or advocate for anything, things would just stay the way they are, which is pretty much the way all of us up here — myself included — want them to stay? That's the question.

I didn't hear many other voices speaking out, either in the community or in the larger, more empowered world, on behalf of the Yaak's roadless cores. So I started stepping up my efforts, publishing even more information about this oversight and asking for help. I made my decision, even though I suspected that the news of yet another significant place in peril might bring onlookers whose ephemeral visits could occasionally, like a brief rainstorm, compromise the peace of the hermits such as myself, and the grizzlies, the wolves. (There aren't many trails in the Yaak, and fewer vistas, in these dense woods; as far as human recreational opportunities go, a beer at the tavern and a burger at the Dirty Shame about covers it.) Still . . . *tourists?*

It's not a beautiful valley, really, to many visitors: it's dark and rainy and snowy and spooky. (This fall, we've had only four days of sunshine out of the last hundred.) The locals can be unfriendly and there are many biting insects, and much fog and rain and snow. Unlike most places in the world, this is a great place to live, but not much to visit. My worst fear nonetheless is of a wave of yuppie acquisition, the gnawing, consuming contagion of looking at a landscape and thinking, *What's in it for me?*

And yet: to be quiet, about injustice? Either answer seemed a hard one.

Tourism is not the answer for this ragged place. The group with which I've started volunteering, the Yaak Valley Forest Council, has been working for many years, trying to get some small timber sales of dead and dying trees, conducted from existing road systems, set aside for the handful of loggers who still live in the valley, and to give the local small mill owners first right of refusal on those logs.

It won't change the world. It won't save that culture. But it will buy time, which is almost the same thing. Nothing lasts forever.

Many of the woods workers are scared to death of me: frightened, and angry. They think my desires for protected wilderness areas in the last roadless cores that still remain would only be the beginning. They believe that the government would then begin evicting them from house and home, devouring the entire community in that fashion, as the old clearcutters once devoured whole mountains up here.

So I'm caught now between two worlds in that regard, as I was once caught between fiction and advocacy: working for the last few bands of independent loggers and mill owners, and working, still, as ever, for the little unprotected wilderness that still remains. Moving back and forth, here and there, in the worst combination of both restlessness and weariness. Believing fully that there is still room for both.

What I like about the notion of wilderness designation is that I could stop fighting, year after year, on behalf of roadless areas. I could go back to my other life — if it still waits there for me. I don't think backpackers would flock to the Yaak. It's not like the rest of the West. It's a swamp — a biological wilderness, not a recreational wilderness.

If it's like this for me, in my soft, privileged life — stressed between the two sides of a question, and the two lives — what must it be like for the grizzlies and wolves?

A young woman who had the great fortune to have been born here, and to grow up here, once asked me that question, the one about being quiet or about speaking up. About being inactive or active. She was upset that I'd said the secret name of her home, my home, to the larger world — the name of this valley. She wanted to believe, I think, that things would stay the same, and that voicelessness, not voice, was more honorable, as well as more prudent.

She didn't agree with the abuses of the past either, but wanted silence, just a little more silence, in the moment. I guess she assumed the future would take care of itself, or that the future turnings of the outside world would avoid the valley, or would maybe even take care of things on the valley's behalf.

And maybe they will. But it has not been that way here, in the past. My experience has been that the future devours. It does not protect.

This is not a place to come to. But it is a place to protect.

One year has turned into twenty-one, and counting. No one I respect could stand by and watch a beloved landscape be damaged without raising a voice. My body and spirit are battered by twenty-plus years of the struggle, but my resolve is undiminished, firm and steady.

I would still like to know that these last roadless cores can be put out of harm's way, forever.

As soon as that's achieved, I'll get real quiet.

I'll walk into the dark woods and sit down.

I don't know what I'll feel. But I know that day will come. I just know it.

5

The Community of Glaciers

I HAVE BEEN THINKING for the last few months, off and on, about glaciers. Burned out, I think, on how slow change has been in coming to northwestern Montana, how little progress we have made in preserving the last few remaining roadless areas as wilderness, and at how resistant we've been as a culture to reforming our forestry practices.

The common definition of a glacier is any patch of earth where snow remains year round, with a depth of ice accumulating across time. But a glacier isn't just a chunk of ice, static, unchanging. It's like a river sliding through time, up one valley and down the next, with the laminar grace of wind or water. What interests me is the point at which a glacier, having invested decades in patient endurance, finally gains enough overburden to metamorphose into a slippery, living fluid and begin flowing down the mountain, carving a new world, setting new rules.

I used to have a certain vision with regard to environmental activism. I used to think that it consisted of the tedious, enduring stonework of a mason; that the activist's duty, in such a situation — outnumbered a thousand to one — was to stay calm and to endure; that even the greatest and most skilled artisan could never be anything more than a laborer, laying down steppingstones in some river across which those who would come later might pass.

What I think now is that it is not like laying stones across a river, or stacking one's words and deeds in an ongoing, eternal rock wall. Rather, it is like being snowed upon in winter. One's life is not nearly so significant or dramatic as a rock wall but is instead far more silent. What we really are is windblown snow, swirling, beautiful yet ephemeral when measured flake by flake.

We activists would like to think of ourselves as hundred-pound slabs of mountain: square cut, durable, useful. But now I think that the opposition — those who would kill and eat the wilderness — are the stone weight and we and our works, however passionate, however intelligent, are but snow, melting in poor years though in good years beginning to accumulate in ridges, drifts, mounds.

For a long time, nothing happens. It's just snow: silent, beautiful, monochromatic — or so it seems. Twenty feet might fall in the mountains one winter; by summer's end, nineteen feet might have melted. But then winter — the time of beauty, the time of work — comes back around again. Twenty feet might fall again, and once more, beneath summer's broil, nineteen feet might vanish. Nothing is happening yet. It's just a bunch of old, crusty snow and ice. But something is getting ready to happen.

Depending on slope and aspect and density — usually a function of moisture content — it takes some sixty feet of ice to make a glacier come to life. Once the proper load weight is established, the glacier begins to move — begins to flow continuously, behaving now as a plastic or a liquid rather than as the brittle solid it had heretofore been.

Some of the ice at the bottom of glaciers has been found to be 25,000 years old. What must it feel like for the glacier as it finally comes to life?

There are so few people up here, and so much land. Although our grizzly bear population is the most endangered in North America, our black bear population appears to be doing all right; there are more black bears than people, more owls than people, more elk, more coyotes, more ravens, more moose, than people.

I know of many in my community who support the idea of wilderness designation for the last little islands of roadless land in our valley. Such are the ingrained social pressures of this corner of the world, however, that it is hard for a person in the valley to dare to admit that desire: the need, the yearning, to know that a few wild places will remain forever wild in the valley, free to grow old, rot or burn, grow young, then grow old again, in a forest's natural cycle.

For several generations the timber industry has been pushing the fear button, prophesying that if roadless lands in the natural forests are designated as wilderness, the landowners next to those forests will be evicted.

So nobody says the W word. We talk about bulldozers, hunting and fishing, the basketball playoffs; but then sooner or later I'll mention the W word, just to keep the idea of it from being forgotten. Everyone will get all upset for half a year or so, threats will get made, names called.

My neighbors try to make it easy for me. I've had conversations of varying lengths (some very short, it's true) with almost all 150 of them at one point or another in my twenty-one years in the valley, and I don't think it's inaccurate to say that roughly 99 percent of them would agree: they'd like to see the valley stay just the way it is and keep the roadless areas roadless. But why call it wilderness? they ask.

Because I'm tired of fighting, for one thing. When I moved up here, I used to be a fiction writer. I loved that craft, that calling. I've had to all but abandon it, to speak out instead for another thing I love now just as much as language — the woods. These woods. I need them to be designated as wilderness because, frankly, there is only a small handful of us up here paying the dues, fighting back sale after sale in one unprotected roadless area after another. By and large, there's not a lot of marketable or accessible timber in these last roadless areas — it's why they never had roads built to them in the first place — but all I can surmise from recent activities is that they — industry, and Congress — want it all.

In the past fifteen years, there have been at least seven

timber sale proposals in the Yaak's last roadless areas; each time, public opinion has been able to turn them back for a little while longer. Things are better for now, but . . .

These are stories that most residents of the valley aren't aware of. They look out their windows every morning, or drive up and down the Yaak road admiring the view, and they tend their gardens and live quiet lives and wonder, I know, *What's all the fuss? Why does this Bass guy like to fight so much? Can't he see that things are better — that logging practices are improving, and that for the most part the Forest Service is leaving those roadless areas alone?*

Of late I get the feeling that my neighbors are growing weary of my inability to take the olive branch. What would you think about calling it a natural area instead of wilderness? they ask. Or how about "heritage forest" or "roadless core" or "primitive area" or even "national roadless monument"? What about "National Recreation Area"? How about an eighteen-month moratorium? How about a ten-year cease-fire?

To all of these, I have to say no, it's not enough. I have to stand my ground, asking for wilderness, which is the only complete and permanent protection a forest or a watershed or a mountain can obtain. All the others carry various loopholes for helicopter logging, snowmobiles, motorcycles, gold and silver and copper mines, hydroelectricity projects.

I'm not saying that I'm against those activities, or even that I'm opposed to them being executed in the national forests in certain places. All I'm saying is that I need for these last little roadless islands will be protected, permanently. I don't want to keep traveling down to Helena or Missoula or Washington, D.C., week after week, year after year, to turn back the roads from those last little refuges. I want my life back, and the frustrating irony is that most of my neighbors want to offer me my life back — if only I will discard my beliefs. If only I will think of myself, and the present, and sell out the future, which is so suspect in any event . . .

As long as there is ice, and snowfall, there is hope. Once the adequate load has been achieved and the ice begins to flow, a second kind of movement occurs, at even greater depth. The glacier itself begins to slip from its contact with bedrock, sliding like a wet tennis shoe on ice. You can imagine, once this phenomenon is achieved, how very hard it would be to stop it. You can imagine how the glacier would begin to write its words, its sentences, its stories, in stone, with claws of ice, upon the previously implacable mountain. You can imagine how such etchings might finally — after thousands of years — begin to get the mountain's attention.

These glaciers, lying so patiently upon the stony, intractable mountain, will in the end have their say almost completely: they will carve and shape and scour all the way down to the core, the bottom, cutting the mountain itself.

In 1874, in Switzerland, researchers proved that a glacier moves not like a grinding, ground-eating tank but with the grace of a river, complete with eddies and currents both lateral and vertical. The scientists pounded stakes into the ice at fixed points, then watched as some of the stakes crept downslope, still upright, as if nothing were happening, in patterns and distances different from the other stakes. By 1878 the stakes were stretching out to form a tongue, and in only four more years they had stretched into an intricate ellipse, giving away the telltale movement that to any other observer would previously have seemed static, hopeless. But from a hundred miles up, or across the span of 10,000 years, the glacier must seem like a sinuous galloping thing, sliding across the landscape with an elegant gait, leaving tracks etched in stone and spoor the size of small villages.

Believing deeply in Wendell Berry's advice that "to enlarge the areas protected from use without at the same time enlarging the areas of good use is a mistake," and in an attempt to demonstrate to my neighbors that I care for them and their ways of life as much as I do for wilderness — believing as I do that they, like me, are of the wilderness — I put aside my wilderness advocacy for a while to work with a small local group — the Yaak Valley Forest Council — to secure one of the nine pilot programs authorized by Congress in 1998 for Montana, Idaho, and the Dakotas.

In these areas, a new style of logging would be practiced. Rather than board feet, two new objectives would be paramount: the desired "end result" of the forest, and community participation in the planning process. Loggers would be awarded contracts based on the quality of their work, not the amount of timber they could scalp. The program would also favor the employment of local workers, who would have more motivation to leave the strongest and best trees. The emphasis would be on the restoration of damaged landscapes and watersheds rather than the further invasion and liquidation of healthy ones.

After six months of hard work, our little pro-roadless group, the Yaak Valley Forest Council, was able to secure a much-coveted position in this federal program. The community held several informational meetings, and eventually nine of us volunteered to serve on the project's steering committee. Three of those nine members were pro-roadless advocates, members of the Yaak Valley Forest Council (YVFC) — the pro-wilderness group that had brought the stewardship logging project to the valley. However, forty-eight hours before details of the final project were to be turned in, opponents staged a protest vote, compiling a limited survey that the local Forest Service used to get all but one of our group's members ousted from the steering committee. Then they selected as one of the logging sites a ninety-one-acre unit that borders my property, with a clearcut as the recommended prescription.

Our group decided to go along with the hastily reconstructed downsized committee in order to bring the project to the valley — and from there, we've limped forward with it, trying to find common ground on these projects, logging units and land management prescriptions on which we can all agree, on which we can reach consensus.

I had very badly wanted to be part of the pilot project. I had wanted to walk through the woods with my neighbors, saying, *Let's take this tree. Let's leave this one.* Like them, I wanted to have a voice.

I still believe that in the Yaak there is opportunity for sustainable forestry. The valley has been turned upside down: it was once 50 percent old growth, but in the past half-century the rampant clear cutting and the taking of the best trees instead of the weakest have converted the valley to a young forest of overstocked, crowded, weaker trees; across the West, nearly two-thirds of the forest now consists of trees less than seventeen inches around. There is much opportunity for the restorative work of thinning, both commercially and precommercially.

Even after the YVFC brought this new logging project to the valley, opponents of wilderness continue to spread rumors that I am against all logging, and furthermore, that I want everyone — myself included — evicted from the valley. Wearier if not smarter, I have retreated to the far perimeters of the valley for now.

Maybe it's part of the glacier's process, to lose some of your fire. Or for the nature of the fire to change under pressure of time and distance traveled, or not traveled: so much labor, perhaps the better part of a life's labor, with not one single gram of tangible difference. It is not a giving up or even a wearing thin, but a reconstituting of desire. In some cases, fire is too quick an instrument for the work that needs to be done. Ice is the tool that is called for — the ice of decades, or of centuries. If you cannot attain speed, even in your best efforts, then perhaps you can gain solace from images of power: the great sheets of ice that sculpted many of the wild places we find ourselves fighting for; the great masses of snow and ice that scribed their direction into every ravine and peak and cirque of these stony landscapes, and which laid to level the resistant landforms, entire mountain ranges of obstacles.

In my various defeats, in my static or backwards-moving attempts at my goals, I have been taking solace in crevasses — cracks in the zones of tension that are created as the glacier creeps across irregular terrain. Though they may reach as deep as 150 feet, for the most part the crevasses are merely cosmetic expressions of the struggle below, and as such, insignificant in the flow of things. The plastic flow of the glacier remains relatively unperturbed. You think things are moving very slowly or not at all. But you must not forget the shiftings and releases of built-up hydrostatic pressures, little understood, whereby one day the glacier surges like a skater free and clear, traveling as much as 180 feet in a day.

I take solace in the agony of the glaciers and their sloppy detritus, their tortured yet elegant residue. A glacier rasps, roars, grinds, hisses, gushes, and spurts its way down the mountains. It spreads before it, like the rimed breath of some advancing colossus, the clattering terminus of boulders deposited as till and outwash. Sometimes this terminus has been carried vast distances, and once deposited in a new land, the deposits can play a truly significant role in transforming the physical landscape. Fire is what we notice, but glaciers are what change the world.

Our lives, our values, are a constant struggle that will never end. There can never be a clear victory, only daily challenge.

After the glacier passes over, all it will leave behind will be sentences and stories written in stone, testimony not to winning or losing but simply to what path the glacier took while we were here, and whether we were the mountain or the ice.

6

Wood

In activism, one frequently hears the metaphor of climbing mountains, or even of climbing one particular mountain, with the repeated assaults on it so continuous and steadfast to the activist that he or she, over the course of a career — if I may use that word not to indicate the trade of time and skill for money, but rather trading the fat sweet middle of one's life, the marrow years — comes to learn intimately the essence and being of that mountain.

It comes to the point at which a kind of clairvoyance is created, with every contour of the mountain so known to the climber that the shape of the climber's brain might begin to reflect the shape of the mountain. The mountain's rhythms and pulses become the moods of the climber, and transfer to the climber a different kind of logic.

By learning ever more about the systems, responses, and processes of that mountain, I believe that the activist comes to learn things of the mountain's past, present, and future that could not be known otherwise, and for which no record or testimony might exist.

Like a hunter long familiar with his or her woods, who comes somehow to know where the quarry might be taking refuge, and who wanders a seemingly convoluted path that nonetheless eventually takes him or her to the exact place where hunter and quarry will intersect with such synchronicity that in retrospect the confluence will seem foreordained — the hunter sometimes even dreaming the night before of the manner and circumstances in which the kill will occur, so the next day, or the next, it is not that the dream seems like life, but that life seems like the dream — the activist too can envision success, but simply does not know what path will lead to that end, or how long the journey will be.

Still, the hunter — and the activist — knows things: interior, unmappable things.

Like the great hockey player Wayne Gretzky, who said that he didn't skate to where the puck was but instead where it was going to be, the activist can sometimes see and know all the pieces, can clearly in his or her own mind see the dream fulfilled — the summit reached — and yet if too much time elapses, the dreamer can be stranded, like a mountaineer in the fog: existing too long in the dream and not long enough in the real world.

You know the mountaintop is up there and yet you cannot quite find your way there, even though in your dream-life you have already been there for many years, on top of that mountain looking down at all the beautiful sweeping valleys below — some of which appear green and lush, and others of which remain still shrouded beneath early-morning rivers of silver and blue fog.

In that middle land — long possessing the knowledge and vision of the summit, even while not yet having gained that summit — you can panic, can become forever lost, can burn out, spending that most valuable of commodities, *passion,* uselessly in the fog, wasting it on dead ends, and on the kindling and nurturing of fires that were in the end irrelevant in gaining any of the paths, or the one path, that would have led to the summit.

You can become lost and fatigued, and in that fatigue and confusion, things can seem suddenly inverted, so that you might perceive that up is down and that there are a thousand ways to fail while there is only one way to succeed, whereas all your life previous to this point you had understood the opposite of this to be true; that the only way to fail was to quit, and that all one had to do to succeed was to keep climbing, for behind such sustained passion all paths would ultimately converge at the top.

And in that climbing-the-mountain model, there comes a point, usually mid-journey, at which it seems that one slogs through the proverbial frustration of two steps forward and one step back, or two steps forward and two steps back, and then even, for long stretches of time, one step forward and two steps back, until it begins to appear that all the previous ground one had gained on the summit has been lost.

There will even be those long and discouraging dark days when one suspects, and then is convinced, that the issue, the cause, would have been better off had the activist, the mountaineer, never engaged it in the first place.

But what if there is some truth to this horrible perception? It is not a truth that will hold — I believe any work that has enduring passion as one of its hallmarks cannot help but drive the issue a little farther forward — but perhaps for a little while, during those dark despairing days, it is true that there *has* been a setback, and not just an ordinary or "natural" slippage or reversal, but one that has your fingerprints all over it.

But perhaps even this is foreordained, or at least so strongly required as to seem foreordained.

Past that midpoint, that fog bank — and it is always out there, in any life, and in any quest — up becomes down; the world is tilted, and will always tilt further and again.

With such middle-aged or mid-careered knowledge, how then does one proceed, with passion and energy waning and the clock winding down? Having given the cause your very best shot and still having come up empty; and knowing not just of your ridiculous failure — your heart was wrong in its youth, you could not save the world, nor could anyone — but also of the terrifying sandcastle collapsings of the crowded, fevered world.

Perhaps it's a kind of supreme self-denial, but it's never occurred to me — on my own — to question my authority — indeed, my obligation — to work as an environmental activist, loving, and using, the natural world; or rather, the world that often lies these days beyond the reach and paths of man. Other people have expressed confusion or puzzlement upon learning that I used to be a petroleum geologist working on private lands in the Southeast, or that I hunt deer and elk and wild birds, or that I support logging in certain places. My clamant desire, clamant need, for some protected wilderness in the Yaak Valley of northwestern Montana — where I live, and where no public land has ever been permanently protected — sometimes doesn't jibe with some people's conceptual images of an environmentalist.

I sense — believe — that those folks would be much more comfortable if someone less imperfect was laboring to protect those last fourteen little roadless areas — pristine yet tiny gardens, really, in the larger scale of things, but vital, still, to the ecosystem. Well, hell, I'd like to have someone less imperfect doing the work too. But he or she isn't here yet. I keep watching and waiting. I — we — really could use that person.

In the meantime I tend — or try — not to get too high-minded, given my own awful and immense and incredibly human complicity in the sinking, or the burning, of the earth. One of the worst things about environmentalists, as has been noted often, is a growing humorlessness that afflicts them — us — and that can grow a little more intense, a little more bitter, year by losing year.

What gall it is, I know, for me — or any of us — to convert to the heart of a conservator and then to allow ourselves to be overwhelmed by the magnitude of the inescapable costs of the presence of each of us. I can find no sustainability in the human condition — yes, we've got to wean ourselves from fossil fuels as quickly as possible, but to buy a shiny new metal-and-plastic hybrid vehicle and call things even, or even good, seems to me in some ways every bit as dangerous a perception as the one that asserts our natural resources and great evolutionary luck (and no matter whether designed or random) are infinite. We are huge, immensely unsustainable, and are destined — for as long as we survive — to displace other living things, and to disrupt or interrupt or even eradicate certain other life processes. We do, however, get to choose to some extent what to honor, in our clumsy and consumptive journey — what to seek to acknowledge, as we plow through the world — and how to behave. Which is, I think, where the environmentalism comes in for each of us, paradoxical as it may seem to some, in light of so much evidence to the contrary.

Being ecologically imperfect, and yet lobbying for wilderness most of my adult life now — well, maybe I can rationalize that seeming contradiction, then, with notions and concepts of honor, and the dignity of effort. But here's another: why wilderness? Time and again I come back to one simple answer: it is the passion that is in me, and it is my home. It is the shape of my mountain.

Maybe it is a kind of giving up and sticking my head in the sand to not dedicate all my days to battling the energy lobby that is camped out in Dick Cheney's bunker, or to work in sub-Saharan Africa, or with population and birth control advocates in China, or civil rights activists anywhere, and to instead retreat to home — even as, increasingly, the battle seems to be advancing on that same home, with so many of the ills of the world, ills we once viewed as foreign injustices, present everywhere now among us.

It's the question for any young person of passion — where do I find my meter in this incredible and exciting journey? What is the shape of the mountain that most draws one's heart, and how long will the journey be? The passionate young person may have found his or her subject at an early age, or the subject may have found the young person, no matter. The real question becomes the meter, the dispensation, the burning of one's days, and — always the trickiest part — the balancing of passion and intellect, logic and intuition, emotion and strategy. No wonder so few, if any, ever make it all the way to the top. Little wonder that the only worlds that ever get changed are the ones inside us, and — sometimes — the worlds of those nearest to us.

But first, oneself. Sometimes it is a matter of holding on to the raw innocence and power and uncompromising intolerance of injustice that one possessed as a young person, but tempering it with kindness learned along the way. Other times it is a matter of losing those things and then, mid-journey, having to go all the way back and look for them again. And hopefully being able to find a place and time where such things still exist.

I don't mean to suggest that in retreating to the refuge of my garden — the tiny million-acre island of the Yaak, which exists like one powerful shining cell in the arterial bloodstream of the once-upon-a-time wildness that stretched, and might yet stretch again, from the Arctic tundra in the northern Yukon down to the farthest reaches of Yellowstone, and beyond, hundreds of millions of acres of the sanity, logic, balm, of wilderness, and the radiant and uninterrupted grace of wild things — I have yet learned balance or meter, or that I have found or attained personal peace.

I still lobby on citizens' energy week fly-ins, still tread (while our democracy yet allows this earned right) the halls of Congress, despite not having the increasingly requisite briefcase full of dollars. I've been working on community conservation projects in Namibia and British Columbia, and on mining issues in the Cabinet Mountains. I haven't yet found a fully logical rhythm and focus, and I still find it easier to say yes than no when a friend or associate asks if I would like to ride off to war with him or her. I do it partly for the friend and partly for the issue — the rhino, the salmon, the bears — and partly because I sometimes feel it would harm something in me far more to say no and walk away than whatever damage the war itself might inflict.

But I do it less and less now, for it is increasingly vital to me that my girls, in their growing-up years, know a father who is somewhat at peace. It is increasingly important to me, in their growing-up years as well as my advancing own, to regain at a personal level a little of that bright space around me. It is a task that, once the personal tipping point is crossed, can become harder each year.

Back in the fieriest part of my life, the black-hole anger-sump of watching one clearcut after another march across the garden of the Yaak, I wrote an angry book critical of that destruction.

Mills began closing around the region not long after *The Book of Yaak* was published. That book had nothing to do with the mill closings; it was simply a personal anger synchronous with the destruction wrought by unsustainable logging, and the awakening breath of what is referred to euphemistically as "the global market" — a polite term for the action of other countries beginning to liquidate their wildlands at the same pace with which we once liquidated our own.

But as the mills in Lincoln County began to topple, I found myself, for reasons not fully understood, pulled into the efforts to try to keep them alive: particularly the local independent mills. Perhaps it was my geologist's background, or hunter's background, and my comfort, or at least easy accommodation, with being a consumer of resources. For how can I, who lives in a wood house, and who has cut firewood for money as well as for my own use, and who has logged for hire — contracting, at various times, half a dozen different loggers — turn my back on and wash my hands of the human consequences of my actions, my criticisms, my voice, and my needs? How can I offer criticism without proposing alternatives or solutions?

To me, it is not the criticism that reeks of hypocrisy — for none is pure — but instead the failure to dream or imagine a solution. The failure to dream at all.

I sense more every year that my real meter, and my real demon or fit in the world, is not fighting for the last mountains and the last grizzlies. The plight of those things is instead an injustice I happened upon while traveling down the road: a side journey, a side path. What should have been six months' diversion, or at best a year's, has become a life. My real meter was, and some days I sense still is, writing fiction. It's one of the hardest things in the world — a thing at which you can fail ten thousand different ways. You have to be daring, and dream of boldness, and yet with a single misstep, a single false thought, you fail. It's my passion, and yet year after year and now decade after decade — nearing the beginning of the fourth decade of my personal war up here — I am kept from that meter by the endless meetings, endless strategizing, and endless, frail connections of thin hope, the dogged hope and faith that this thing can be done.

And despite the maddening nearness of the goal — the paucity, simplicity, and moderation of the task — to protect as wilderness each of these last little roadless areas in one little million-acre Eden — and despite the frustration of one connection and possibility always leading to another, ripple-like, I suppose the eternal limbo of a seemingly infinite array of connections that have never added up to anything is better than the benumbed alternative: the fragmentation defined by disconnectedness, and the absence of connections.

Still, even as we continue to make connections in the strange and often frantic world of activism, the connections beneath us drift ever apart, as if on shrinking ice floes: the populations of autumn-run westslope cutthroat trout becoming separate from the populations of grizzly bears, which are becoming separate from the populations of whitebark pine, which are becoming separate from the populations of Clark's nutcrackers . . . It occurs to me that the populations and communities of man are also alarmingly, maybe irrevocably, adrift, due to the usual contributing factors, fear and its byproduct, anger, even blind hatred — and that is a most troubling problem indeed, one that I think makes the protection of our last wilderness areas all the more critical.

For me, wilderness areas are a place to walk into, while I am still able, and to rest — a place where the ever-dramatic and ever-increasing problems of the world are always, gently and miraculously, placed back in their divine and proper scale — and upon my reemergence, I always feel better equipped to deal with them.

They are a place that absorbs and tempers my own fear and anger, a place for restabilization. If I go into them joyous, I return joyous. If I go into them fretful or angry, I return becalmed. What magnificent alchemy, magnificent grace, is this? Given that each of us is here for only a very short time, what huge value is this? Surely it is immeasurable.

Even as I am laboring, thus far with futility, to protect those farthest forests from the last reach of man, I find myself turning back to look at those lands we have already logged, those lands we have already zipper-stitched with roads — and while I see, on every walk I make, public lands that can and should be restored to wildness, damaged lands in need of rehabilitation — I also see forests that are injured, crippled, compromised by their affluence: young forests, typically, from which the cleansing, nutritive recycling benefits of fire have been excluded.

Someone came into some of these forests forty or fifty years ago, mowed them down, then walked away: and in the old forest's place, weeds sprang up.

So I am not just an activist who uses wood, sometimes knowing where it comes from and how it was harvested, and how its harvest fit into the community from which it came, the community not just of men, women, and children, but of trout and elk and bears — though at other times, not knowing. I am an activist who wants the logging to continue, who sometimes looks at the forests near a community — *not* in the wild backcountry, or the wilderness — and thinks, like a hunter, like an extractor, like a consumer, *Okay, I'd take* that *tree, and that one, and that one.* And I imagine then, with pleasure, the increase in water subsequently available to the remaining trees, and greater ease in reaching that water, and other resources — the rich mystery of the scheming, seething soil, the secrets of which are still so little-known to us — and the remaining trees' greater access to that requisite moisture, in an ever-drying, ever-warming world.

In the old days, nature was allowed to be more selective, burning some but leaving others. Insects too would pass through in waves, setting up the next fire, as would windstorms — but such movements, like the orchestral sweep of music, were tempered, conducted, logical. They possessed the grace of wilderness. Maybe it is simply my oil man's background, but just as it bothers me — makes me edgy, jumpy, to be in a remote piece of backcountry and to know it is not protected as wilderness — so too does it bother me increasingly to be standing on the outskirts of town and see small trees that should still be growing dying instead because there are too many trees and not enough water. Trees dying not from logging, but from an absence of logging.

When I go out on the ground in that neighborhood space immediately around human communities and see the dying and drought-stricken trees, I believe in cutting, and in using wood to build homes, to sometimes heat them — sometimes for ceremony, other times because no other means exists — and to make paper and books: recycling those materials, of course, for as long as is possible. I don't believe the zero-cut folks are right. I like the contrary logic, that logging — securing usable wood from certain places in the frontcountry — can help protect the farther backcountry. But then I see the government taking good science and corrupting it, and I want to throw up my hands and quit and say, *Forget it, if you can't log it right, don't log any of it.* Even the mildest logging, if not done with exceptional care, can tear up the soil and bring in weeds. *Forget it,* I sometimes want to say, *just walk away and leave the woods alone; let them all die, let them all burn. Things will probably balance out again in a few more thousand years.*

But each year, for whatever reasons — stubbornness, or the wretched spark of hope — I am lured a little further on, daring to dream for just one more season, or one more year, that we can still cobble together a workable plan, a solution. Each year, the solution seems so close, so graspable.

And each year, the Congress, or this-or-that certain congressional and presidential appointee, retreats, lies, obfuscates, reverses; and every year, there are short stories that go unwritten by me; and a life passes by.

I love the scent of the gas-oil mixture as I funnel it into the saw in advance of and preparation for a day's work — the shuttered shafts of gold light spilling down through the forest — and I love the slow, syrupy dolloping of bar oil into the crankcase.

I love the snug fit of the saw tool over the hex bolt, love the muscular resistance of the starter cord, and the gurgle, the burble, of the engine catching. I love the choice, the selection, the belief that what I am doing will improve rather than harm the area where I am working.

I love the humility that attends the taking of a tree's life, knowing you may be making the wrong choice but that you have thought about it and are doing your best.

Later on, in the mill, I love the scent of sawdust, and even the shrill sound of the buzz saw, ripping and planing. I love the clatter of boards being stacked, the new-cut wood brighter, before it begins to oxidize, and never seeming more filled with potential than in those first few days after being milled.

Don't get me wrong. I love trees — standing trees — and a big old giant rotting snag, riddled with woodpecker holes, with a marten peering out from one of those cavities, and with its base apron-scorched from past fires, or even fallen on its side onto a bed of lush-emerald carpet — is the very best: but I like a board now and again too, and I like a tight-grained floor of one-inch strips of fir, polished smooth underfoot in the kitchen.

It's okay to be an environmentalist and use wood; it's okay to consume oil but to be humble in one's consumption, and remember to seek out, and demand — and use, where possible — alternatives. It's okay to eat food, seeking out and choosing, where possible, the healthiest meat, healthiest vegetables. It's okay to be alive.

What isn't okay is to fail, as stewards, to protect a piece of the world's great puzzle: a still intact, and still wild, ecosystem such as the Yaak.

I believe intuitively — and the more I learn, the more I believe scientifically — that any creative solution to the tasks and challenges presented to us in this million-acre garden must have as one of its components the permanent protection of the last, wildest gardens-within-the-gardens — the preservation of those remnant and ultimately ungovernable sparks of wildness that, like the innocence or purity or passion of a young person, will hopefully always inform our other actions, and the people and communities we are always on our way to becoming.

And in such gardens, and from such gardens, might we, and our ponderous hearts, be better suited, in that tiny solace and brief rest, to reconsider, and address with greater resolve and with greater strength and creativity, some of the more vexing problems of the world, such as where we get our energy, and — perhaps interconnectedly, or perhaps not — how we treat our neighbors? Not just our neighbors across the sea, but our neighbors down the road?

Increasingly, I find myself gripped almost daily with the fear, the suspicion, that we — humankind — are becoming quickly less perfect, that we have gotten in over our heads, have gotten dreadfully lost on some much larger mountain, and are behaving badly, behaving selfishly, behaving foolishly: and that worst of all we are heading down, not up. It's just an intuitive thing, but it's strongly felt.

Again, I think that if I stopped to really consider or ponder it, I could easily find myself plagued with — hypnotized by — indecision, given my own complicity in this massive imperfection and web of contradiction: sometimes merely perceived, though other times — so often — rock-solid real.

What kind of environmentalist am I, really, to still be using petroleum, and to still be using wood? Almost nothing, really, with regard to our huge presence in the world these days, is in the least bit sustainable. This certainly doesn't mean we shouldn't do the best we can. I think what it does mean is we shouldn't be high and mighty, and should never forget the unaccountability of the awful and immense cost of the joyous gift of us being here — and again, while trying to do as little harm, or even as much good, in those areas of our lives where we are most active and passionate, it may be perceived there is a sin or paradox here, to be desiring perfection and absolute sustainability even when it is not possible, and to likewise be advocating for the protection of pristine country even while seeking elsewhere to more actively manage and manipulate the fringes of an ecosystem — though I do not see a black-and-white contradiction but instead simply another part of the mountain, one that is perhaps rarely visited and hard to get to, but without which the mountain would be shaped differently, and less appealing, less mysterious, and less inclusive of our presence upon it.

The ecologically naughtiest among us — a beef-eating, oil-guzzling, chain-sawer — should still be able to need and desire the permanency, in some places, of wilderness: the ecological gold standard of grace and logic, even as we continue to so often, and so spectacularly, fall short in the pursuit of those qualities.

I do not see paradox in anyone striving for those things — but after twenty-plus years in a timber culture, I sometimes question why I like to cut wood so much. It's good to step back now and again and look at the larger silhouette of the peak. And then in the morning go back to the mountain and to decide, each day, step by step, which route to take.

It has not yet occurred to me to not keep climbing, and when I am on the face of the mountain, I try not to look back too often at my, or anyone else's, imperfections or contradictions, but instead keep striving toward the vision of where I want to be, and what I need. It's the most we can ask of any species.

7

Oil

BEING AN EATER OF oil — a consumer — is surely the worst of my physical sins, one about which we can all continue to make rueful jokes between shrugs of acceptance, always hoping or even promising to do better another day. But the bleeding continues and no one man or woman can staunch it — choosing a Subaru wagon over an SUV will not stop it or staunch it; my off-the-grid home with its bank of a dozen solar panels will not repair it. The world is bleeding ten million barrels per day, is burning ten million barrels of black crude, pouring those invisible carbons into the sky above us. We are not just burning holes in the thin sky membrane that protects us from the fierce love, fierce focus, of the sun. Some days I imagine that we might be crushed beneath such invisible tonnage of carbon, all that exhumed and combusted and exhaled carbon pressing down upon us in ever-ponderous overburden. It is hard to imagine, as we are driven, pounded down into the ground under the weight of our own affluence, pounded and pressed down to ankle-depth, then knee-deep, waist-deep, shoulder-deep, then gone — hard to imagine, finding ourselves now beneath such detritus, that we might somehow manage to keep housed within our chests the bright spark of hope or faith that inspirits us as a species: the ability, even at this dire point, to dream and glide and laugh and love, and to be fully human, fully alive, fully burning.

How dare we imagine, at this late stage of consumption, that some force, some tide of change, might miraculously choose to reach down through our overburden — as the geologist's drill bit probes the dense shell of stone, searching for the ignitable oil below — and yet find and then ignite that secret buried remnant spark, the tiny flame of who, on our best days — in days gone by — we once were, a culture of givers rather than takers?

And when the bleeding is all done and the oil is all gone — not just the peak oil, but all the oil, down to the last drop — and we lie buried beneath our history, still waiting for some greater salvation or redemption to ignite us, to retrieve and direct us or move us toward another path, another world, another heart — even then, another temptation will reside beneath us and around us: if not the fluid supple allure of oil, then the densely compacted chitin of coal, the old dirty brown Paleozoic swamps, each lithified like a charred heart into brittlecake seams of strata — ten thousand years' worth of such brittlecake. And I fear that it will be the easiest thing in the world then to simply remain buried in this land of the fossil fuels, and to continue gnawing at the coal, worsening our problem tenfold with every sulfurous exhalation, and with the now acidic celestial dome or dark curtain above raining sulphuric hail, mercuric tempest, brimstone.

To such a future, do I continue to try to write pretty little vignettes about wandering the pastoral or even deeply wild meadows, the hills and mountains, chronicling a sweetness that I know will one day soon be gone by, and in so doing enabling that future reader some ancient and reverse vicariousness, the particular rapture of fantasy known to some readers in some readings? The fantasy of once upon a time?

Chronicles from a time when there were still grizzlies and wolves, a time when one could not travel far without seeing moose, badger, elk, coyote, lion, even wolverine. A time when there were still four full and balanced seasons upon the land, and a time even when — despite the usual small-town mix of differences, misunderstandings, paranoias, and even enmities — there was somehow, at some deep level, some dim reminder of connectivity, still, here and there, a few places that had not fully been broken apart, fragmented as if into spider-web shatter, and places where people recognized these connections, and worked as best as they could to help hold together or keep intact that which had not yet been broken away. To staunch that drift, that outflow, to conserve and nurture that which was special, rare, and, again, valuable.

This maybe is where my unusual life as poet and oil man, novelist and logger, environmentalist and elk hunter, twines to form a braid that sometimes feels even to myself, long familiar with it, to be shimmering with paradox: for there might be some solace in writing such fresh, clean, sweet, and even beautiful little poems and stories, and, on occasion, there might even still be some honesty in presenting the world — this world, or this corner of Montana — in such fashion.

To that brimstone future — a future that I fear will be too much characterized for the first time at some profound level by the absence rather than presence of things, unstoppable though I fear this juggernaut is now — do I write of the dangers and day-to-day disappearances, or keep writing instead of the curious and perhaps unvanquishable spark in my heart to still perceive beauty, even amid cascading ruin and rot?

I cannot shake the feeling that it is somehow we in this moment who possess a greater responsibility than all the sinners who preceded us — for never before have the imperfect been so charged with the clear knowledge of the consequences of those wrongs.

Surely there has existed since the first dawn or spark of consciousness in all men and women a realization of the divide, the mountain pass, between right and wrong. And in this regard it is somehow we who, like perverse pioneers or trailblazers, first crossed over some high rocky pass, needle threading our way into the next new valley, passing over some tipping point that had never before been crossed.

Again and again, this is my fear: not so much of our being judged in the future as having been the last generation to possess the potential and the possibility — even if hugely diminished by the trajectory, momentum, and infrastructure of all the generations that preceded ours — to effect change of the most profound kind: not a change in knowledge, but in entire systems of logic, or even further, changes within the heart.

That's a lot to ask of any generation, or any person, but I'm not so much worried about whether I, or we, will or won't beat that rap. Instead, my fear is that in perceiving that ours might be the generation that failed to stop the last wave — the wave that had been building higher and higher — certain interior things are also at risk.

You can risk losing some of the bounce in your step, you become more cynical, more apathetic. You accept loss, failure, injustice. You forget rage, you forget rapture. You become less sensate, then insensate. You become lost, as the wild country that once inspirited us becomes lost. You become less humane. For that too we might and should be judged by the future. Did they remain human, the future might ask, or did they give that up too?

Or might not even know to ask.

The trouble with any generation, I realize belatedly, is that it always passes so damned quickly.

I often wish I could stick my head in the sand and ignore how huge each of our rich American footprints is, knowing of the way our hypocritical black hearts must harden still further each time we make yet another purchase, travel yet another mile, or casually avoid letting yet another injustice touch our hardening hearts — blocking out those knowledges, laying more necessary scar tissue over the truth, or delaying our redemption, our conversion, until tomorrow, or the next day, or the next, and delaying it further, then, to the next generation, as have all generations before. Writing off this heavenly paradise as a sour loss, discounting and depreciating as capital losses the vanished miracles, the endangered species, the going-away glaciers and icebergs, and slipping into the heated, toxic, sulfurous vapors of the future not as if cast there by any fierce and Old Testament judgments but as if such a place is really, after all, where we deserve and, worse yet, somehow desire to be.

Who am I, who is any of us, to dare to protest the state of things when, on a relative scale — America versus the world — the footprint or sinprint of even the most virtuous among us is but a shade of gray's difference, really, from that of some stogie-puffing cow-eating whiskey-gulping oil company CEO in a ten-gallon hat with a two-gallon mind?

The only options, then — with all of us so impure — are to give up and accept our continuing failure, or to try to preserve the rarest and most valuable things and buy a little more time, just this side of oblivion. To not give up hope. Giving up on any of these ventures — securing energy independence, or forest sustainability, or wilderness preservation for our rarest, wildest places — and instead accepting loss, failure, extinction, oblivion, is not yet an acceptable belief, and so I personally choose the model of attenuation: trying to buy time. If we cannot sustain ourselves for another ten thousand years, then can we not at least try to sustain or preserve ourselves — to buy back time — and stretch a hundred years of our future into a hundred and fifty, or a hundred and seventy-five?

I have to believe that if we act now — finally — we can buy enough time to keep searching for answers, or rather, perhaps, to begin the slower process of implementing the answers, many of which are not really so difficult. Sustainable technologies — particularly in energy independence, which is to say, national security, thereby wholly altering our (and the world's) relationship with the Middle East — already exist; the answers have already been found. We are just treading water, and killing people, and being killed, until we decide finally that the costs are high enough to put those other technologies to work.

Likewise, in the vexing area of water dependency — another issue over which wars are already being fought — technologies and answers exist. And yet we continue marching — hurrying — toward the vent holes, the fumaroles, from which is issuing the sulfurous elixir. We know the consequences of our trajectories and yet push forward, more headstrong and obstinate than ever.

Sometimes I imagine this book being read by people fifty or even a hundred years distant, not as popular text by any means, but as obscure dust-covered museum-like memorabilia, a curious and extremely local place-based document of natural and social history from the turn of the century. Such a reader might wonder, What were the people of the twenty-first century like?

I imagine such distant examiners wondering about this

with the curiosity of social anthropologists. What were their sins, what were their mistakes? Were they oblivious to the history they were forging, the path to the cliff's edge they were blazing, or did they just not care, or could they just not help themselves? Were they a weak people, or strong? Did they have morals, or were they hedonists? What was their typical day like? Were their brains and sensory perceptions different? Did they have a God or just the name of a God, and what did they worship?

And a hundred years from now — in whatever strange and heated and sometimes horrible, and sometimes wonderful world — might any of these emotions find resonance with them?

To such a future, I announce, *Here are my own sins. I speak for no one other than myself.* My primary sin is that of middle age; the sin of moderation, of not winning the most crucial battle, the one we have always waged and will always wage — the battle for habitat, for territory: what biologists refer to in all species as "the territorial imperative" — the hard-wired gene for conquest.

We know we must take back and restore clean air, clean water, and wildness — the grace and logic of remnant cells of health — but we are not winning this battle. And here in middle age, I find myself speaking — as if possessed by the enemy — of common ground, compromise, creative solutions, different paradigms, and hope, rather than trying despite being outnumbered a hundred to one simply to run the sword through the next infidel.

It is of course because we have all become infidels.

The list of my sins is perhaps in some ways slightly different in scale, larger than some, smaller than others — but is surely all of a kind, at this point in history. We are all complicit, and hence we are all obligated — authorized — to act.

Did they not know? I can imagine other, subsequent generations asking (as my generation sometimes self-righteously inquires of previous ones). *Did they not care?*

The answer is yes, some of us knew, and yes, some of us cared. But the momentum of our trajectory is overwhelming. We sense that things are going poorly, that something is slipping away, and yet the force of habit is powerful.

It — the future — is almost out of our hands, if ever it was in our hands.

Still, we have to begin somewhere, if we are not to quit, to give up and roll over: and a handful of us in my little mountain valley has decided to start in the obvious place — within the forested walls of the valley and within our own hearts too, in which hope still remains, despite the latest round of directives and revisions offered up to the land by George Bush the Second, in his reckless plummet through time.

My sins then are those of anyone. It's possible that I spend some small amount of time more engaged on battling these issues than the usual sinner, but if that's true, it's because there is perhaps no one more blessed than I am with the privilege of inhabiting the edges, the borderlands, of this great unprotected and quickly vanishing wilderness. And while part of what I hope to offer is a solution, and motivation for executing that solution, I also wish to bear testimony, in this whirlwind era of loss, to what I have seen and what I have felt; and to hope that to those readers of a hundred years distant, these sentiments and emotions will not seem too unfamiliar.

I hope that there are some areas in the Yaak Valley protected by then, and in a strange and bittersweet way I also hope there are still some areas left that are worth fighting for, despite the taxing, grueling nature of that endeavor.

Experience, as well as landscape, has certainly shaped me, as it does each of us, and under the experience category — how I came to be — my life in the West has certainly been influenced by my first life, in which I was a petroleum geologist in Mississippi.

What a wonderful life of gluttony it was, of passion and appetite serving in unfettered confluence with the imagination. To leap into vast treasure vaults buried miles beneath the surface, wandering in one's mind over terrain no human had ever seen. Dare I say that there were times spent mapping that approached the spiritual as well as the ecstatic? In such maps I was not serving the pursuit of riches — my salary was not tied to success or failure in such explorations but rather simply in showing up each day and doing my best — though in other ways now I wonder if such lack of remuneration was not ultimately a blessing, in that it allowed me to indulge in a kind of academic or intellectual purity: hunting for the sake of the hunt, and as such willing and able to dream big. Able to pursue without forethought of failure, unrestrained by the need to play it safe. Able to inhabit, in my mind, a fantastic wilderness without bounds — and not just at any one fixed point in time but at any point in time, on any level of strata.

And though such things did not consciously enter my mind as a young man, there was surely at some level, some depth, the understanding that no matter how successful I and my geology compatriots were, there would be no end to the hunger, the appetite, for that which we discovered: that the world would always be willing and eager to purchase and consume whatever we could bring it.

And in that system of logic too there was a kind of absolutism and purity, for better or worse.

Using oil as if it were water, or air, or like nothing at all: that was how our world was back then. We knew we were going to run out one day, and sooner than some expected; but as for all the other stuff — the now obvious stuff — we did not see it coming. The first widespread public pinpointing of global warming came in my opinion with Bill McKibben's 1991 classic, *The End of Nature,* though the hypothesis as well as evidence had been buried out there for at least three decades prior to that, and — astonishingly, in a pre-9/11 world — we were not yet connecting the dots of geopolitics in order to realize that the most insecure thing our country could possibly be doing was to buy energy from another country.

We knew we didn't have enough oil, but somehow we thought everything would turn out okay, and that when we really needed something — the ancient hydrocarbons — we would always be able to figure out a way to get more: as if our desire alone would be sufficient for such alchemy.

What a different world it was back then! Mine, I mean: working in Mississippi as a geologist, slipping into and then through those strange Republican halls of power — the energy traders, or, as they called themselves, energy producers; though we were not that, the energy was not created by us, but rather merely discovered. As my wife, Elizabeth, the grammar policewoman, drily corrects our daughters when they inquire, "Mom, can you make some corn for supper?" there is, of course, up until Monsanto's genetic tinkerings, no way to make the corn, or the venison. "Only God can make corn, sweetie," she'll say. It's a rejoinder I would have liked to have known back in the old days, telling Mr. Cheney (who even then, with his friend George, was at play in those underground fields of stone) when he, and they, referred to domestic energy production, "Only God can make a barrel of oil, Dick."

There is a finite amount of it, it took a very long time to make, they aren't making any more of it, and, as with most valued things — except, perhaps, for passion — it is a thing more to conserve than to spend.

For my own part in this particular national or global sin, I have tried always to "produce" or find more than I've used, and like to believe that I have; but that does not mean that my life is sustainable, or that anyone's is. The game is rigged;

even with my bank of twelve solar panels, I won't get out ahead, and again, this all points back to why we should protect what little wilderness we are still fortunate enough to have.

It does not matter to such places — or to the grizzlies, lynx, and wolverines that still inhabit them — whether the despoliation by people like you and me is intentional or accidental, or somewhere in between. It does not matter to those places and those inhabitants whether the loss and fragmentation, the homogenization, and the march of endangered species into one extinction after another are met with the hand-wringing lamentation of Democrats or the jubilant bloodlust exultation of red-meat Republicans who persist in being worried about various forms of civil union even as the world burns.

And likewise it does not matter to those wild places and those inhabitants whether those who seek to protect their continued existence in the world are pure or impure. Biology and survival are so impure in that regard — so passionate, so clamant, so absolute — as to approach a kind of incandescent purity.

Where I hunted for oil and gas — where I learned to hunt for, and cherish, mystery, in the first years following childhood and adolescence — was not on the public lands that each of us is responsible for safeguarding and passing, intact and complete, to future generations, as the previous generation passed them to us, nor the special wild places near and within the Arctic National Wildlife Refuge, nor the wind-swept and heart-sweeping Rocky Mountain Front, or the magnificent Front Range of Colorado and Wyoming, or New Mexico's fabled Otero Mesa.

Instead, I was old school, working in the Southeast — in little hidden basins in north Mississippi and Alabama, mostly, often prospecting among farmers' soybean fields — lands privately owned — or, occasionally, in hardwood forests atop hogback ridges, where we would cut a thin lane through the forest, laying down a corduroy board road for the trucks to travel on, before pulling up all those boards, like rolling up a carpet, upon completion of the job and leaving the farmer's, or woodlot owner's, little lane of light to quickly close back in. We would seed it with clover to return nitrogen to the soil.

Still, I do not mean to profess innocence or purity. There is more impurity in me now, each time I start my car and drive somewhere, than there was then, twenty-five years ago, when I drilled those tiny boreholes down into the farmers' fields and discovered the oil and gas.

As a geologist, then, and a discoverer of our second-worst addiction (our worst being apathy), how can I possibly dare to argue for the protection of our last American wilderness?

How can I possibly not?

8

The Poison of Language

NEXT TO VISION, I believe language is our strongest sense. It can tap directly into the imagination. Like a lever and fulcrum, it can move almost anything. It becomes a kind of vision. To one who loves language, and who loves wild country, imagine the fury at seeing the two loves pitted against each other: language being used like a wrench to crack open and suck out the last good and vital marrow of a thing. The corporate manipulation of my craft.

As a writer and reader, I believe in the power of language, of how even the slightest tweak in a short story can make all the difference to that story: just as in wild nature, where the slightest tip, slightest recombination of essentially the same basic elements or atoms, yields dramatically different results. To one so attuned — to the intangible, qualitative nuances within a wilderness or to the subtle meanings and cadences of language — it is all the more maddening, then, to see the corruption of language used on behalf of those aspects of our culture that would destroy wildness rather than seek to preserve it, and which, even when we seek to use nature rather than destroy it, do so with disrespect rather than with respect, forbearance, consideration.

It's a platitude that big business runs the country, and frankly, whenever writers do battle with the monied interests, we expect to lose more than we win. But we like to think that as writers at least we can help shape the future, if not the present, by creating a purer, textured, mythical world in which the right thing is done, the right decision is made, and in which dignity, beauty, and nobility abound.

We're not. If anything, too often as writers we're losing these battles of the future, the battles of language and the evolution of the culture to come, even more decisively than we're losing the money wars. And as readers, we're losing these same battles every time we accept unquestioningly certain deceptive turns of phrase — language that seeks not to serve or preserve but to take and control; language of secret selfishness rather than generosity.

Just as the forest is being taken from us, so too — like an echo, or perhaps a foreshadowing — the language of the forest is being taken from us — insidiously, slyly, steadily — and we are being given instead, are accepting, unthinkingly, the language of machines, and the language of the sick and the diseased. There are individual words being used daily in the battles over wild country — and which have been used for many years now — that cede vast amounts of wild territory each and every time they are uttered. Language that is multiplying hourly, obscuring the true beauty and possibility of believing that there might be a few landscapes that can do just fine without the curse of all our help or knowledge. "I want to speak about the forests," the poet W. S. Merwin has written. "I will have to speak in a forgotten language."

Prescribed treatment. Implicit from the very beginning in this notion of a prescription is the statement that we are the physician and that nature is sick. This is not to say that there are not places where traditional natural processes ("historic vegetative patterns," in the parlance of the management agencies) have not become slightly, temporarily unbalanced as a result of our past mistakes and transgressions — nor do I think that there aren't places where we can "manipulate" the forest to bring it closer to what most of us might describe as "health." But we use the phrases "prescription" and "treatment" for every cutting unit on the national forests. If one's goal is to help preserve the sanctity, mystery, awe, and power of wild places, the battle is already half lost every time we open our mouth.

As a longtime resident of a logging culture, and as a weekly respondent to project after project, I am every bit as guilty of using that same language — and not only in my letters of entreaty and outrage, but in my own thinking as I walk through the woods. Instead of seeing a fallen, rotting, orange, mulching "nurse log," I see diseased trees, pathogens, fiber "wasted," and value that is not "captured" in a timely fashion.

Instead of seeing the mysteries of mycelium, I see root rot and dwarf mistletoe, and my mind skips ahead to the obvious "application" — fell the fir, girdle the larch. Stop the progress of death and dying. Stop the creation of new soil.

When a lot of trees in the wilderness die for one reason or another, and fall down or blow over, why is it called "fuel loading" rather than, say, "a bounty of carbon"? How did we lose even this battle? Is it the forests that elicit from us this exceptional deviousness of language? At first I think that it is; but when I ask the grassland activist George Wuerthner if he's noticed similar abuses of language in the prairies and desert, he responds quickly with his own litany of complaints. "When the BLM is putting taxpayer money into developing water sources, etc., etc., on public wildlands to benefit cow owners, they call them 'range improvement' funds. The only thing being improved is the ability to raise cows. Another similar choice of words is 'partnerships.' 'Partnerships,'" Wuerthner says, "is usually code for the taxpayer to pay the money to get some exploiter to do what they should be doing anyway. For example, we see 'partnerships' all the time with farmers, where we pay for vegetation filters, unfarmed areas used to trap the sediment away from highly erodible lands that shouldn't be farmed in the first place because the non-point pollution exceeds clean water standards. But rather than enforce the law, we have 'partnerships.'

"Of course," Wuerthner continues, "there is the mention of grazing as a 'tool,' as a way of justifying livestock use of the land. There is the division of 'Wildlife Services,' which serves wildlife by killing it. There is the Conservation Fund, which pays for the eradication of prairie dogs with federal dollars. A very good 'conservation' of our wildlife."

Still, most of these grievances seem to be a degree less insidious, "merely" converting the poetry of science into the brute nouns of big business. It seems to me there's something more sinister in the language used to disassemble the forests, and I can't help but wonder if there's not something in the nature of the landscape itself that nurtures in us this deceit. Maybe it has to do with our deep-seated instinctive fears of the unknown — and that in a landscape of diminished sightlines, we are more inclined to be fearful. Again, is language in this instance a substitute for vision?

Wuerthner points out more forest-related abuses of language. "There are the insect 'epidemics,'" he says, "and 'outbreaks,' which simply describe a normal periodic population process that affects many natural systems. These insect 'pests' are 'destroying' forests," he grumbles. And since he hasn't even been preparing for my question, he too clearly has been doing some serious simmering about it. "We even see it with regard to hunting," he adds, "where hunters don't kill wildlife, they 'harvest' it. Well, I don't harvest deer or elk, I kill them, and I'm quite willing to accept the proper term instead of hiding in some farm terminology."

"Catastrophic" fires? Why not refer to past political administrations — those of Bush, Reagan, and others — as catastrophic events? We use these terms freely, back and forth, in our dialogue with the agencies, but would we ever have the temerity to suggest that postindustrial management of the public lands has been its own kind of "catastrophic" event?

Who defines for us what language to use, and what language not to use, and when we may and may not speak? In a true democracy, and amid true freedom, would we still be making these choices for ourselves — with the stories we tell, and by recognizing when language comes from the heart versus when it is just trying to sell a product?

I fear increasingly that even as the wild country around us is being compromised, like beach sand crumbling at the touch of the waves, so too is our language of wilderness crumbling beneath us, until one day our country will have forgotten how to even talk about grizzly bears, and wilderness, or any of the other vanishing things and the shadows, the stories, they cast.

I have been arguing, lobbying, pleading, on behalf of the last roadless cores in Montana and the Yaak for so long now that I rarely use the word *tree* anymore, using instead the more familiar term *timber,* whether the trees are still standing or not. Dead and dying trees are usually called "material." Even the relatively benign phrase "woody debris" sounds like something you might comb out of your dog's hair after a hard day of hunting: an annoyance, a nuisance. Often when there's a lot of dead and mulchy, crumbling logs in a stand (delicate fairy slipper orchids growing out of that soft duff and powder, as well as a richness of mushrooms), the official agency language will speak of how those groves need "sanitation."

How funny. It's in these tangled, structural, unsanitary places that I often like to sit and rest, mesmerized by the intricacy of deadfall and blowdown, secure in the faith and belief that in such a forest, even what looks to me like unstructured chaos, there is surely grace and order and design. I cannot name it or prove it or even see it, but sitting there in its midst, I can feel it all around me.

Something is being lost hourly, daily, by this course of events, and I am not sure what to do about it or how to slow or stop it. I see a catastrophe of language, a catastrophe of authority, a catastrophe of arrogance.

What positive words or turns of phrase stand against this trend, this turning? What original thoughts or older traditions can counterbalance it? *Independence* and *freedom* are two words that come to mind, but we have not yet successfully connected — in our minds — those values and words to the wilderness.

Order, grace, logic are some of my personal favorites, though again, it seems sometimes that we aren't succeeding in asserting — in showing — that these are the natural words to be used in discussions concerning natural resources.

Many days, the losses in this battle over language are as basic as the differences between a language of peace and a language of war.

The power of language is like the power of a map, which, when you lay it down on the table, tends to clarify and stimulate and, best of all, concentrate the imagination. It possesses nothing less than the power of a dream or a vision, and yet words bridge that land between the abstract ether of vision and the physical, tangible, elemental world of stone, antler, feather, forest.

I want to believe that the people who use language most effectively will have the greatest influence on the imagination, or the dream. And I want to believe that the language of generosity will triumph over the language of treachery and greed.

Clearcuts of course are no longer called that. The old guttural Anglo-Saxon phrase has been replaced with the sinuous, almost lisping "seed trees with reserves" and, most comfortingly, "shelter belts," which, again, sound more like some sort of individual retirement account than a forest.

Engineers speak of the road "prism" as they make plans to enter the last roadless cores in benign fashion — the word *prism* conjuring not only the stability of the pyramids but, more subtly, the friendly kaleidoscopes of one's childhood. Where are the slaughterous runoffs of spring beneath that word *prism;* where are the crushing fragmentation, sedimentation, slumpage, and collapse?

What are the cumulative effects of such usage — this daily refashioning of the woods' identity into a thing that not only can but should be always, always, controlled and manipulated?

How much room remains in that kind of language for what we all know we are running out of, which is wilderness?

Where I live, *wilderness* is sometimes like one of George Carlin's "Seven Dirty Words" you could never broadcast; you have to often take a deep breath and gut up for a moment just to say the damn word.

What can I do to help change this?

How much time do we have left before it becomes a moot point?

"Regeneration harvest"? I'm reminded of a scene from the movie *Raising Arizona,* in which the bank robbers storm the bank and tell all the customers, "Throw up your hands and freeze." The man named afterward in the credits as "First Hayseed" looks puzzled and pauses before saying, "Well, which is it, young feller? You want us to put up our hands, or should we freeze? We can't do both . . ."

"Shut up!" shrieks the bank robber. "Raise your hands!"

I think I'll just keep using the word *clearcut.*

What are the consequences of a language that does not properly respect its subject?

This crumbling, this fragmentation of awe and respect for wild country, is certainly nothing that scientists can factor into habitat-effectiveness ratings, and yet I believe it is as real and significant a cumulative effect, a stress, upon the ultimate future of the wilderness, and its wild inhabitants, as might exist.

Let the last few wild places escape the curse of our language and retain their eloquence. Let's keep the last precious bit as it is, rotting and burning and regenerating at its own pace and rhythm: a place where bears can be most fully bears, and where poets can be most fully poets, and even a place, perhaps, where scientists can be most fully scientists. I continue to believe that our dwindling wilderness areas remain surely one of the greatest available textbooks or source books on the true possibilities of language, story, and the imagination, as well as character — both in individuals and collective communities — as well as the greatest living sanctuaries on earth for our long, long list of threatened and endangered and sensitive species. For a variety of reasons, including the health and rejuvenation of our language and stories and imagination, we need to protect and preserve the last dark forest gardens, the last few unprotected public wildlands. But please, let's don't go in there and "ecosystem manage" them.

Sometimes it seems as if our language is becoming as fragmented and manipulated as the dwindling wild landscape itself. How can this possibly contribute to democracy, liberty, or personal or national freedom?

I want more, not less, of the kind of landscape that instills in us always the remembrance that the wonders of life can exceed even the finest reaches of our language. We have enough, more than enough, of the chained and roaded, paved-over and cut-over lands, so subservient to our short-term hungers. As for the last few wildlands we have remaining, we can never re-create them after they are gone or altered. We can only protect them, and treasure them — or, as an alternative, tell stories about them after they are gone, with the echo of an older, and now less familiar, even forgotten, language.

9

Fourteen Gardens

I LIVE IN A DARK WOOD where the elegant icy blue shadows have long since impressed themselves hard upon my heart. This is such an astounding valley, rich almost to excess in so many ways: productive and gentle and filled with soft-shaped mountains that resemble lying-down men and women. The valley — the Yaak — is easy to love: rich in its four distinct seasons up here on the Montana-Canada border, and rich too in the cast of wildly eccentric human characters who have scattered ourselves here and there through the forest. But the Yaak is richest of all, I think, in the diversity of life forms that are found here. It's a place of anomalies, and opposites, and paradoxes — or rather what seem at first to be paradoxes but which really are each other's half sides of the whole.

It is this latter richness — the fullness of opposites — that gives the valley such a feeling of completeness, and from that sense of fullness there emerges a resonance that is palpable even to a visitor.

Always, in this valley, there are two things where in another valley, or upon another landscape, there might be only one. In this dark, low, forested swampy jungle of a mountain valley, the shadows of things seem as real and distinct as the "things" themselves, so that sometimes you can't really say which is shadow and which is shadow caster. It's not just the way the mountains blend in to the fog and clouds of the Pacific Northwest, but something less noticeable, and less definable. Things have not yet been decided; no one thing or way of being is dominant, and everywhere, in so many patterns and examples, it seems to me, there is the sensation of unfolding, of birthing, and of all the other vigorous processes of life.

This valley has the living dignity of extreme energy and enthusiasm — a vigor of such magnitude that we're conditioned, I think, to view it as excessive, when all it really is is complete. Nothing's ever gone extinct here, so that this valley is not yet a fraction of a place but is still its full and whole self. Which is a way of saying, I think, that even in the valley's shadowiness, it casts shadows back.

•

What is rare in much of the rest of the West is common in the Yaak. Rather than having one tree species dominate the canopy — for example, lodgepole pine — the forests of the Yaak are likely to share the canopy equally with several other species, the tops of giant larch neck and neck with Doug fir, or even Western white pine.

A giant cedar, which is a moisture- and shade-loving species, might stand shoulder to shoulder with a giant ponderosa pine, which is typically a lover of dry, warm sites. And amid these two opposites there might be others — the deciduous, softwood colonies of birch and aspen towering nearly as high as, and sharing that space with, spruce and hemlock, so that the forest type cannot be said to be any one thing — which is precisely, of course, what gives the Yaak its oneness: the oneness of a complex and complete diversity, a oneness of earned and competitive tolerance rather than exclusivity.

Because this wedge of a valley (it's shaped like a thick heart) exists in a unique seam between the northern Rockies and the Pacific Northwest — possessing, for the most part, the landscape of the former but carved and shaped by the weather patterns of the latter — the Yaak holds in its heart this two-storied-ness, this double richness.

Not just south-slope wildfires, but north-slope fungal rot. Salamanders and ice; frogs and glaciers. It's all still twined together up here, a glorious thrumming creation. And while it's true that nothing has quite yet gone extinct up here (I know of no other valley in the Lower Forty-eight for which this can be said), the Yaak's fullness is deeply imperiled, for so many of those rare animal populations are down to but single or double digits. (For that matter, there aren't but about 150 people who live up here year round. Canada borders us to the north, Idaho's spiny mountain wall of rock and ice to the west, the enormous manmade reservoir of Lake Koocanusa — ninety-plus miles long — to the east, and the Kootenai River to the south, curved like a bow to receive the arrow of the straight-running Yaak River, which drains this valley into the larger world.)

In this strange shadowed land of two-ness rather than oneness, all the various species somehow manage to find a place, to make a place, and sometimes to share a place. When one species goes up on a mountain, the other will often come down, so that their movements of accommodation act like the pistons of some unbelievably powerful engine. Or if not a machine, then a larger living organism, or a story.

Because nothing has yet been decided, there is very much the feeling, the belief, that there is still room for everyone, for anyone. For one's true heart's beliefs and desires.

How do you make any decisions at all when everywhere you turn there seem to be twice as many ways of being, twice as many options — either of which, it would seem, can honor the landscape and its myriad diversities? How do you seek or carve out a fit in such a place — or rather, how do you accept the carving? Which strokes in that carving do you accept and which do you reject? Is there any choice? Do you have any say in the matter?

For a long time now, I've been an environmental activist up here, working hard for two basic causes: to promote local and sustainable small-scale selective logging practices rather than the industrial clearcuts of the past, and to seek permanent wilderness designation for the last fourteen little roadless areas up here, the last fourteen little wild gardens where we have not yet built logging roads into the furthest and farthest heart of the forest. Fourteen little gardens, ranging in size from 1,000 acres to 38,000 acres. Fragments and crumbs.

Throughout all of this wild valley — it's nearly a million acres, with 97 percent of it public land, belonging to no individual or corporation, but to every American — there exists some of the wildest and most biologically diverse country in the Lower Forty-eight, and yet Congress has never allowed even a single acre of it to be protected as wilderness.

Does the forest, and those fourteen little gardens, desire to be protected? Something in me knows better than to claim that it does. But I know also that I feel fiercely, with every fiber and ounce of a sense of justice in my heart, that such protection is right, and necessary, to preserve the fullness that typifies this valley.

People have been real quiet about this forest, the Kootenai, for a long time.

It hasn't helped.

Easily a million loaded log trucks have rolled out of here, carrying the logs — and the jobs — away to distant and indifferent mills. Often I'm shamed by my moderation in the face of what's being lost and the dire lot of the threatened, endangered, and sensitive species that rely on those fourteen little gardens for the survival of their race in the world. Only fifteen or twenty grizzly bears left; only a dozen mated pairs of adult bull trout. Only five or six wolves, and a handful of wolverines, and a handful of lynx. Only one remaining population of pure-strain inland redband trout, holed up in the last uncut basin in the upper part of the valley. One occasional woodland caribou. One. The last officially verified sighting was in 1987; the last unofficial, in 1989.

A thing I've noticed about my own heart, in the last few years — after so many seasons of loss and anger and bitterness, and with the scars of community polarization lacing themselves across my heart like the roads that rip up into the tops of the mountains, roads that carry noxious weeds and loud machines and dozers and chain saws into the last gardens, and that funnel mud and gravel down into the rivers during each spring's runoff — is that I'm becoming less bitter, that indeed, I think I'm losing some of that anger that once burned so steadily in me, and with such incandescence.

I'm not entirely comfortable with this waning and find myself puzzling over it often, wondering if in this softening I'm letting down the wild places that have for so long sustained my spirit. I want to be a good warrior, durable and dependable, speaking always clearly and calmly in my own voice and no other's in support of my views on justice and against actions that I perceive to be unjust.

It's one of the activist's oldest and most heartfelt laments: without justice, how can there be peace?

How much of my slowing down is maturity, however, and how much is fatigue? And worse yet — worst of all — how much of that slowing down is me ceding to injustice, and to silence, merely for reasons of personal comfort: because I might be tired or made lonely by that incredible road map, the latticework, of the hatreds hurled at and carved into my heart?

Often these days I find myself stopping while on a walk or a backcountry ski and staring off into the forest, puzzled, almost as if consciously asking the forest for an answer or a clue, some counsel as to what is transpiring within me, and why, and whether it is "all right" — whether my occasional softening and slowing of pace are still loyal or fair or just.

I'll stand there, watching some slant of light or some patch of snow or some dark shadow cast by a tree trunk, and wait for an answer; and when none comes, I'll turn and walk on, or ski on; and in that moving on, I'll imagine sometimes that I feel a little distance growing, like the subtle rift of an icebound fracture line along an avalanche slope, high in the mountains late in winter — though other times I'll feel a bit of the distance close back up, like the knitting of cracked or broken bones, or the binding of lichen to damp stone.

Sometimes I imagine that I am strong and indefatigable, and that this valley is vulnerable and fragile, in need of support, human support, and compassion and fairness and beloved celebration. Other times — increasingly — I'll imagine that I'm the bent-over, ailing one in need of tucking in beneath its wing for a while.

I look out at the forest often and try to figure out what evolving pattern is going on, and why I'm feeling two things these days rather than the one thing I felt so resolutely when I first started out up here, which was to fight, fight, fight, fight. Sometimes when I am staring at any certain patch of woods up here, asking that question, I grope for the easy lesson, the easy pattern. I tell myself that my activism, my fiery soul, is like an old river cutting ever deeper, or like an old forest slowing in its growth but growing ever stronger and more stable. Or that my heart is like the sleep of bears, which rest for six months of the year beneath the snow and ice; or that my heart and desire for justice possess the patience of glaciers — intractable and sometimes inscrutable, sometimes creeping and other times retreating, but always forceful and desirous; or that my heart and my work on behalf of this valley are like the migrations of the wild ducks and geese, going away for a while but always returning, always, with unshakeable fidelity.

I think my occasional pauses and restings, these days — the eddies existing where once there were none — are perhaps most like the comings and goings of the migratory animals.

Which is confusing, since I consider myself so much a resident of this place.

Perhaps my coming and going is like the seasonal movements of the deer and elk (and of the lions and wolves that follow them): rotating from the shady cool north slopes in summer onto the sunny south-facing slopes in winter.

For a fact, some sort of rotation is going on, and I am in it — even if I do not yet know fully the name or logic or rhythm of it.

Many days I long mightily for a new young activist, or a handful of them, to come drifting in, to enter that volcano. I know these are not the generous thoughts of a truly strong leader, or even a warrior, but many days I feel them. I try to neither embrace those thoughts nor push them away. They just come on, seemingly on their own — or, who knows, perhaps flowing in from out of the woods.

I suspect it is unwarriorlike to even be admitting such weakness, or if not weakness, then softness. How hard it is to let go of the thing you once viewed as a strength — rage, and tenacity — and not feel that the underlying commitment is reduced, or that your efforts are made somehow less effective by the absence or diminution of that rage and ceaseless freneticism.

Sometimes the navel-gazing gets even worse. Sometimes I will find myself wondering if the near ceaselessness of my campaigning has not somehow been counterproductive. Sometimes I wonder if the thing I desire most — peace, and a solution that accommodates all the different desires and needs of this region, peace within the forest, and peace within the long-warring human communities that live at the edge of it — is not somehow conflicting with my cause.

Perhaps it's merely a symptom of shell-shocked activist-fatigue, but often lately it seems that the harder I work, the further behind I fall, in these goals — peacemaking, moderation, and the discovery and identification of places of common ground in the community. It seems some days as if the intensity of my desire casts a shadow that is the opposite, or other, of my desire; or, again (a truly frightening thought), as if my desire for peacemaking and common ground is the shadow thrown by the gigantic force of the despoliation, the quick-buck greed, the inflexible and the non-accommodating way of the other world. Who can say whether the kestrel summons the field mouse, and the lynx the hare, or vice versa? What does it matter, really? And if the answer were known — which is real and which is the shadow — what other choice is there? Silence has not helped this place — has harmed it, in fact — but could I, can I, work smarter — with a calmer, more guarded heart, perhaps?

I wouldn't know how to do that.

And yet, maybe that is exactly what I am learning to do. It would be deceitful to pretend to have a calmer or slower or even smarter heart — but perhaps the mountains themselves are counseling me, even at a subconscious level, to slow down, somehow, and to begin to consider pacing myself, counterintuitive though that may seem.

Perhaps I have been in these mountains long enough, and have become enough a part of them, that they are now whispering to me, *Peace,* or, *Calm down* — as perhaps this same message slides down the myriad canyons and between peaks each night, after all the humans have gone to sleep. Or perhaps they have always been calling out this message to me and I am only now beginning to hear it, and I am so confused by it.

Still, I can get pretty angry. It seems as if the mountains get smaller every day. Even as fast as I'm aging, it seems that the wildness in these mountains is aging faster, disappearing, even more rapidly than my youth.

It is not a question about being noisy or being silent. But could I work smarter? I hate my limitations, and what I perceive to be the boundaries that encroach yearly upon both my energy and my creativity.

The answer seems so god-awfully simple: to protect these last pristine areas as wilderness forever, free to develop at their own pace — to burn or to rot, to grow old and then blow down or fall over and to begin again, in tangled, graceful symphony — and in the areas that already have roads, to log sustainably, and cautiously. And to encourage jobs in restoration — of which there is ample opportunity — rather than in the continued extraction and liquidation of the increasingly rare and valuable public assets: wildness, and shadow, and peace.

Many days it feels as if I have run out of ideas, or options. But like a lost hiker — on snowshoes, perhaps, far back in these tangled mountains — I keep trudging on, one foot in front of the next, on through the deep snow. I'm not even tempted to quit. I'm just frustrated that the end seems ever farther away.

Is it like this for any of the other inhabitants of this place — the grizzlies or caribou, or the last of the wolverines? Is it like this for any of the individual groves of forest, or even any of the individual trees? Must this frustration, and at times this anguish, be a necessary part too of the valley's wildness?

In my wearing down, I tell myself this: that even when the

trees blow over and lie down and begin to rot, they give back to the forest — becoming more productive, actually, in their senescence than they ever were in the vibrant, leaping, clamorous growth of their youth.

A forest needs the mulch of rotting logs at least as much as it needs the saplings and seedlings of new growth, and as much as it needs the young trees, and as much as it needs the big and old trees. The beetles and ants that sweeten the mulch are as vital for the bears, more vital, than any of the bright green needles of growing, living trees. The flicker-pounded cavities in the rotting hulks and husks of tree corpses provide greater warmth and security for dozens of different species of vertebrates as well as invertebrates. In this lush forest, there is nothing about rot that is not good.

And yet . . .

Increasingly, I find that I have a craving. I want more and more to step away from essays such as this one, and from my lobbying trips to D.C. and my volunteer board memberships and leadership positions in various local grass-roots organizations; away from my letters to Congress (even while knowing I will never stop doing this), to return instead exclusively to the crafting and the writing of pretty little stories — short stories and short-short stories — and to make not just long languorous novels but beautiful little poems, and to even paint little paintings, tiny scenes no larger than a sheet of notebook paper, and to make little sketches. I feel this yearning deeply, intuitively, biologically, feel it like blood draining from a wound, and I hope to be able to begin soon. Just a little longer, I keep telling myself; just one more year, or maybe two at the most.

I have hiked nearly all of the hills and mountains and creeks in this million acres, many of them repeatedly, and what I think is that, for one reason or another, things have not yet been decided here: that this landscape, only so recently emerged from beneath the cap of the last glaciers, and poised here between the cusp of the burning West and the rotting Pacific Northwest, is still totally in flux — sun and shadow, sun and shadow, with those dualities creating the larger oneness, a wholeness so complex that I have not yet been able to decipher it, and likely never will. (I think that even the essence of time itself is somehow still in flux up here, in dynamic indecision, with regard to this valley's future.)

I believe fiercely that every ounce of energy counts, so up for grabs yet is the future of this wild place, and indeed, this wild state, and that, unlike for almost every other bioregion, hope still exists for this place — not the distant hope of the future, but hope in the moment, hope now, of preserving and sustaining this place's wildness. I believe that even one more person's small voice, no matter whether strident or calm, can help tip the balance of time and circumstance upon this relatively unpeopled landscape; or that one more poem, or one more certain photograph, or one more small song can help tip the cant of fate toward the preservation of the wild, the thing itself, rather than away, and to the shadow and then mere memory of the thing, as has been the case in so many other places — in almost all other places.

The situation demands that I hurry up and work harder, and so I do, and yet even far within me — like the sound of metal banging or flapping against metal, in a high wind — I hear, and feel, that yearning to slow down and step back; and I do not know what to do except to keep doing both things, the thing and the shadow of the thing — making the pretty little pictures and continuing also the slogging grunt-work of the hardcore activist — until one day, I assume, nothing will be left.

For myself, I suspect there will never be any answers but instead only the awkwardness of the struggle — and the struggle, perhaps, a sublime kind of grace in itself, grace that merely disguises itself as awkwardness. I will keep traveling across the deep snow, with my head sometimes tucked down and other times looking up and around, and from time to time I'll glance off to the side, stopping and looking off into the woods as if still waiting for that answer.

Fourteen little gardens are all that's left. Am I being too greedy, too gluttonous? If I let go of my desire and my sense of justice, will they magically be protected? *No.* Will they magically vanish overnight? *No.*

I want to stop and paint. Why won't I stop and paint? What voice urges me on?

10

Who We Are, What We Do

It's one more brilliant green May in the Yaak, and I'm sitting down to what feels like my ten thousandth article, op-ed, or plain old letter to the editor, my ten thousandth entreaty to this or that senator to protect the last little fourteen gardens, the last tiny fragments of roadless areas left in the Yaak. This green sunrise Sunday morning, up before the girls are stirring, I'd frankly rather eat a mountain of wet cardboard before settling in at my desk.

I've just finished up some op-ed, alert letters, strategy outlines, blah, blah — burning up all of sunny Saturday yesterday — and it occurs to me yet again that this would be a lovely time, an opportune time, to immerse myself in the lost world of a poem, or even, more ambitiously, a short story — my heart's true habitat, I suspect — or even, most ambitiously and gratifyingly of all, a novel.

In my mind, however, there is nothing, and has been nothing for a long time: only the metal-against-metal buzzerring response-and-counter-response of the activist answering the bell yet again. It's long ago become an addiction, and an unhealthy one — I feel my *self* vanishing — and yet I feel that I've come too far on the journey, and asked for too much, from too many, to step aside; nor could I.

Every year I tell myself *one more year.* Just one more year and we'll be over the hump.

Many mornings, I no longer even feel the old desire to enter the lost and lovely territory of fiction — the incredible adventure, incredible discovery and passion, of that terra incognito. But this morning is not one of them. This morning, I feel somehow that I have been suckered by the world, or by industry, and have been left holding the bag, and that it is an empty bag, one which in another life or another path chosen might have been fuller, if not filled, with bright stories and novels like diamonds and gold. And even now, in this twenty-first year, I keep thinking, *This is it, this is the year. One more, and I will be released back to the fields of literature,* even as each passing year reminds me that the zest for romping in those fields is diminished: that although I still love a fine sentence, or a fine story, that great green passion of youth has receded and gone elsewhere — resides, perhaps, in other young people now — so that I would often be as content, I think, to hang out with my daughters at softball (while they are still young), or to lie at the edge of the bright green field and watch them play soccer.

What I mean to be saying is, it's not every day anymore

that I get the old deep yearning to engage with the wonderful make-believe of story or poem, and I'm regretful, then, that on the days when I do, the circumstances of my incarceration — hostage to assisting in the defense of the Yaak — do not allow me to engage with the brief and temporal return of that passion, which was once so central to me. It may be one day again, but not now.

It has not all been loss, however. One of the gains has been the deep and abiding friendships of trust and respect with people I likely would never have known had I remained exclusively a short story writer. I probably never would have become enmeshed and immersed in these people's lives, or they in mine, but would instead have continued on in a life of quiet isolation, with who knows how many extra hours spent poking around on the ridges and mountaintops, creeks and wooded canyons and ravines, countless extra hours dreaming and tinkering with stories about made-up characters and settings, made-up places, made-up lives.

That has been the trade, for the most part — the only thing to show on the balance sheet: these friendships forged by nothing less than enemy fire and siege, by a blind hatred that has surrounded us. Stories gone away or never dreamed, and hikes not taken, in exchange for friendships. It is not what I would have chosen, but who can say that given complete free will, I (or anyone else) would always make the right decision?

I want to believe that I have not squandered time spent with family or that our time together has been in any way shortchanged or compromised as a result of my activism —

that only my short story writing has been lost. A ludicrous wish, I know, and a myth, but one I cling to.

The Yaak should have had a ton of wilderness designated a long time ago. Forty-four years ago, when the Wilderness Act was passed, there were roughly 600,000 acres of unprotected roadless wildlands in the Yaak. It was like a secret Glacier National Park. *That* would have been something to get excited about, and would have been its own kind of interesting what-if path, if taken. Would we be facing 15 percent unemployment in Lincoln County, as we are now? Would the health and social issues be as severe? It's hard to say. It's hard to imagine they'd have been worse.

Instead, the industrial road building and clear cutting proceeded unfettered up here along the Canadian line, completely out of sight and with few residents living in the upper Yaak — only a few dozen, back then, and even now, only about 150. Local activists such as Chip Clark, a timber cruiser who developed a Forest Plan alternative back in the 1980s that would have harvested dead lodgepole rather than big green mixed conifers, were routinely jeered by hundreds at public meetings. In a small town, and a small community, these things matter, for whether you are a hermit or a social butterfly, these are the folks you see every day for the rest of your life, and vice versa; the folks whose children your children go to school with. Under a skewed and destructive, unsustainable system of hate — blind, indulgent, uninformed, bullying hate — in a small community, however, enemies of friends end up being, as if by rule of veto, enemies, and enemies of enemies, de facto allies or associates if not friends. It is illogical, unproductive, it robs dignity from the human experience. It holds a community hostage, which is just the way a few would like it.

It's been forty-four years without wilderness for the Yaak, and twenty-one years without it for me and all the others who have labored and dreamed and desired it for all these years, as that once great landmass was whittled and chopped and shaved and bladed and hacked and hewed, losing about 100,000 acres each decade — Amazon rainforest–type figures — until finally, here at century's beginning, we're down below the 200,000-acre mark.

A few activists began fighting for individual roadless areas in the Yaak, such as Mt. Henry, decades ago, only to see the Yaak acreages — lacking a national, regional, and even local constituency — be traded away in whatever few wilderness bills, or proposed bills, have been able to skinny through one or both houses of Congress. The 1978 Montana Wilderness Bill, which established the Lee Metcalf Wilderness down near Missoula — a critical landscape in its own right, and rightly honoring an utterly exemplary legislator — came down, in conference, to an either-or demand, the poker chip trading in which the Yaak, up until now, has always lost. The environmentalists got one area and the timber industry got another: the Yaak, unfortunately.

Even in a 1988 legislative proposal, which passed both the House and the Senate — a Kootenai National Forest bill, mind you — there was, incredibly, no acreage in the Yaak: Ronald Reagan pocket-vetoed the bill in a successful attempt to place the failure to pass a statewide wilderness bill on the Democrat senator John Melcher, who was up for reelection, running against a Republican radio station owner and auctioneer, Conrad Burns (who, despite being the chairman of the powerful Senate Appropriations Committee, lost his 2006 reelection against the newcomer — and Democrat — Jon Tester).

Such has been the story of this magical, low elevation, inland rainforest: to always be the bartering chip for other losses, and other gains, rather than being allowed its own victory. A colony for resource extraction and liquidation, a political chip rather than a place. A place with unfinished business, and yet a place so productive and magical that even today, after forty-plus years of abuse and/or being ignored, it is still brimming with opportunities, solutions, and clamant yearning, and a kind of wildness that can be found nowhere else in Montana.

It's important to stress that I'm not the only one working for the Yaak these days: far from it. But for a long while here it was pretty lonely. So much so that I'm not entirely sure I've made the transition into realizing it is no longer that way, that year by year, other folks pitch in.

Sometimes I forget that more and more people not only support my passionate views but, amazingly — or so it seems to me — are willing to work for them.

I try to caution them away. I try to tell them what it used to be like, and what it *is* like, in a small community. And yet, they step up anyway, daring to voice their love. *Needing* to voice their love, and to participate in creating a solution.

There can be no denying it: in a small-town timber town — or what was once upon a time a timber town — a series of one-horse company towns scattered throughout this vast county, with each burg remarkably isolated from and suspicious of not just the outside world and liberal-elite environmentalists, but of each other — there are costs, surprising costs, to one's love, and the choices one makes to testify on behalf of that love.

You can, unfortunately, count on sacrificing work opportunities and careers, fracturing friendships previously believed to be solid. You can count on (but why did it have to be this way?) replacing the serenity of a life in the mountains with a life of gurgling-acid sleepless-night activism; on acrimonious private meetings with maddening political operatives; and endless field trips to sylvan glades often about to be trashed, or already trashed. Be certain that no matter how hard you try for it to be otherwise, when you attend rancorous public meetings, it will be with a bull's-eye painted large on your chest.

I don't really know where to begin. It all kind of blurs into a continuum. When I was a child, there was a bully who lived next door whose maraudings were so severe that my middle brother, Frank, began tallying a list entitled "Bad Things Jimbo Has Done to Me."

The threats of personal harm obviously top the list. When I was a child of middle-class privilege growing up in the suburbs of Houston in the 1950s and sixties — skating around the neighborhood sidewalks on steel-wheeled grinder skates that emitted a spark-riven roar deafeningly hypnotic to the skater, which could be heard approaching from blocks away, or playing touch football in the streets, weaving between parked cars, or being tackled on the short-lawn width of those tiny yards, rotating from one friend's "field" to the next as we tore up the turf, week by week, like so many rooting hogs — I had no inkling or imagination whatsoever that I would grow up to be hated, or that my name would be reviled not just among my neighbors but by those who'd never met me, who'd never sat down to ask about my goals or values, and worst of all, who did not know the creeks, ridges, and drainages in question.

I did not imagine I would move from down near the Mexican border all the way up to the Canadian border, and would pass through and live among the mountain and meadow haunts of grizzly bears — a species so endangered in the Yaak as to be already like a ghost: "the walking dead," some scientists and activists have called this population — or that I would live among savage hermits in a gloomy, dark wintry wood, among people passionately hopeful for the overthrow of a government in which they no longer participated. I never imagined as a Pledge of Allegiance Cub and Boy Scout — a possible young Republican-in-training — that I myself would become heartsick over the secret grinding gears of power, the movements and machinations of which followed always only one direction, the path of money, choosing always and only the path that led to the pool, the pit, of the most money, rather than any lesser amount . . .

It's one thing to be threatened late at night in a bar, after alcohol has replaced blood in the body's system. I've stopped going into the bars, not out of any fear, but having come to realize the waste of time: earnest conversations with your enemies who have never met you bear little if any currency the next day. And by and large, the work of the West these days is no longer taking place on the late-night barstools, where hangers-on still nurse old miseries and laments, but instead in meetings with county commissioners, chambers of commerce, public land agencies, congressional staff, and the moderate civic organizations of any stripe who understand that the old indulgent blood lust of the past, the self- and place-destructive drunken brawling and public catfighting, will continue to doom the rural outback to its own kind of self-prophesying ghost town purgatory, rendering a collapse more complete than any of those that they feared the "environmentalists" were dreaming and scheming for them.

It is one thing, then, to be threatened in a bar. But it's another, more disheartening thing to be threatened, repeatedly and across the years, in public meetings; and disheartening, also, for no one — not the agency officials supposedly running the meeting, nor any community member — to speak up and out against such imprecations: for you are the scapegoat, which is a powerful cog and gear of its own kind in any rural fear-built and fear-based community in peril.

It's a system, a model, to which many in the community can become addicted — a time-honored way of passing blame and responsibility and all the fears and tensions of an era onto the shoulders and back of a single individual, or an individual's name. And so fierce and iconoclastic can this habit become — this myth, like one of archetype — that even after you, the scapegoat, have hunted down your enemies, cornered, corralled, and collared them, made peace and broken bread with them, forcing them to see and hear and know you for who you are rather than for who they have heard or feared you are — even then, the corona, the identity, lasts, even among those who now know better, for from a community perspective, it is your identity. It's who you are; it's who you've become. It's like a childhood nickname that no longer has meaning: it's still your name. *Buddy. Red. Fatty. Skinny. Devil.*

What ritual, then, might exist for the absolution or dissolution of such unfair identification? By what process might the mantle of scapegoat be shed, burned or buried, and forgotten, releasing the carrier back into a normal life with the grace of anonymity, or non-hate? None that I can think of, save for the validation of success: the designation of those last fourteen areas as wilderness, at which point the ones who feared or the ones who hated will be forced to see that the world did not collapse but instead went on pretty much the same, and maybe even a little finer, a little smoother, with no more caterwauling sidewalk roar of steel-wheel friction grinding through the community day and night, year after year, decade after decade.

That is the only ritual I can envision or imagine — the

only liberation I can foresee — and I eagerly await that release.

When you are an activist in northwest Montana, particularly in the Yaak, here are more of the little things that you sign on for:

Not only have I become a lightning-rod nightshade dividing-line bogeyman unseen symbol — a spur to some people's imagination, in that regard, as even in their looking back to what they perceive as the glory days, not all that long ago, of hauling out more than a quarter of a billion board feet of big green timber each year. Additionally, these people dare to dream ceaselessly, it seems, of new iniquities, devious secret agendas, that I might be up to, ascribing to me a black-hearted intelligence, a Machiavellian secret grand design so vast and complex as to be almost flattering, were it not for that little part about calling me a liar.

Because I have the gall to ask that fourteen little roadless areas in the Yaak be protected as wilderness — a scattered little archipelago comprising less than a fifth of the valley, in distant upper-elevation regions of little if any timber value — while the rest of the valley remains open to snowmobiles, motorized access on open roads, logging, and so on, people who oppose the *idea* of wilderness present me in the newspaper regularly each week as being against all logging, and single-handedly responsible for unemployment in the county. They insinuate or declare that I and my environmental kind are responsible for the rampant wildfires of a globally warming greenhouse-gas world.

As someone on the front lines who tries to get out into the woods as much as possible, I've been seeing firsthand for some years the cumulative effects of an invisible kind of fire that is overtaking much of the West — drought — and understand that in certain overstocked situations, you sometimes have to cut a tree to save a tree. It wasn't by accident that our group lobbied for, and received, the first experimental stewardship forestry project on the Kootenai National Forest, in which logging work would be conducted by local loggers, with all of the money generated being kept in-county for restoration work — more jobs — rather than being sent back to the federal treasury. Nor was it by accident that in the one timber sale our group has ever appealed among the hundreds that have marched across the Kootenai National Forest (and still, all the big mills have gone away), we went out and found "replacement" volume to substitute for that which we sought to protect (unsuccessfully) in one of the valley's finest views.

It wasn't by accident that our group sat for more than six months, meeting almost daily, to try to find a way to keep the Stimson plywood mill in Libby open. We were faced with the task of finding more timber for the mill: a red herring, as it turned out, for after we found the timber (in the overstocked wildland urban interface), the mill closed anyway. We likewise spent hundreds of hours ground-truthing small timber sales and lobbying for small business set-asides to help keep the sawmill up in Eureka open, though it too finally closed.

I can't help but wonder sometimes if it's like this for other activists elsewhere, beyond the mountain walls of our valley. How engaged should one become? Only a little bit, or halfway, or all the way?

Because we are playing to win, the answer for us is all the way.

When you sign on to be an activist in northwest Montana, people in the grocery store will avoid eye contact, particularly if they're hanging out with outspoken opponents to your views. Forest Service officials — federal employees, your public servants — will badmouth you not just in secret within the closed-door meetings of the agency (instances related to me by others within the agency) but in public. You'll be mocked, criticized, misquoted, misstated by various (some, not all — but all it takes is one) agency resource specialists seeking to brownnose for the very superiors whose own actions and attitudes have contributed to this culture of anti-environmentalism within the agency.

You sign on for more little petty stuff — an unending and unpredictable supply of it — such as the year the supervisor of your forest, when you dare to invite him publicly to go for a ground-truthing walk across a proposed timber sale on which you have a difference of opinion — a postfire "salvage" sale on your favorite mountain, a mountain that by the Forest Service's own plan is supposed to be managed as Class I "viewshed," a mountain shown by the studies of an independent forester you hired to have 86 percent of its trees after the little fire, even as the Forest Service says they all died and must be clear cut — the supervisor (theoretically in charge of community development) publishes a letter calling you a "disservice to the community" and a fabricator. The mountain is logged, clear cut — even after you had gone out and found "replacement volume" to make up for the precious few board feet of timber that might have been "sacrificed" by a lighter treatment upon the land, in that one cutting unit.

Little stuff, ceaseless stuff; decades of stuff. You try to keep your nose clean and volunteer where you can, and be a productive part of those fragments of healthy, functioning community wherever you can — but there are mines going off everywhere and you never know when or where you'll step on one. With one or two rage-blinded ideological exceptions — spit-spraying, slobber-mouthed renegades who very well may be, in the words of one local health care worker, "pathological" — it's almost always the ones who've never met you who dare to bay the loudest.

Little things: not long after we formed our group, a lightning-strike forest fire started in the woods only a few hundred yards downwind from our house, and the local fire department balked and didn't show up. Some young kids working part-time fire crew for the Forest Service came and cut a line around the fire and knocked it back, and everyone was okay.

Big stuff, juicy stuff: a mosaic of car bombs — literally, as one of our supporters found out. Crazy stuff, and all over a ferocious lie that some of the skulkers, the self-pitying oh-the-world-is-against-us ones, require, it seems, in order to keep going each day: so filled with a hate and a rage within that they must have a scapegoat, must hate another with that terrible blackness — the blackness of their hurt and outraged and stunted, tiny hearts, if they themselves are not to be crushed by it, the poison within.

On your worst days, when the unending stream of it is pouring in — when your name and this vast and simple lie, that you hate logging, is being passed around the county as if in some kind of bizarre phone-tree prayer circle, in which respondents from far and near — again, who've never met you or talked to you — are bombing letters in to the little community newspaper, calling your proposals to pass a sustainable forestry initiative in which industrial timberlands will be replanted and logged again rather than subdivided — an open space initiative — a "perversion to the community."

On those worst days, you feel no rancor at all to the hate-filled letter writer, only a brief sadness and numbness before shaking it off and getting on with your life. But then, later in the day, or the next day, what comes creeping in — your own kind of self-pity, like a contagion — is the disappointment not that the lie, the Big Lie, continues to spread, but that the hundreds of people in the community — from the loggers you've hired to work on your own land, to the contractors who've worked on either the stewardship logging or restoration project, to the agency folks themselves who have had their caps feathered by these projects, to the mill owners and mill workers who know that you've been active on their behalf, and the agency folks who time and again have come to you in secret and asked you to try to help broker a peace on one or another lawsuit, to try to get this or that flow of logs released — remain silent.

They remain silent. Every once in a blue moon, when it's really going bad — when the letters are bombing in, and you're sitting on your hands, not responding, not sinking to that level, but instead just taking it — someone in the community will make a little joke about it designed to cheer you up and to remind you who your friends are, to remind you that you have friends, and it's crazy, it's ridiculous, how much of a boost even that one little thing, said not in public but private, will help carry you through the rest of the day. It's crazy, it's amazing, how fragile and puny we are. What hope, really, you wonder some days, do we have of effecting any real and positive change in the world, when in reality we're so puny and fragile?

Little things, pissant things, but again the stuff of hate — hate surrounding you like a bubble, secret rivers of hate winding like lava through the community. Is it the nature of mankind to accommodate such lava and move to avoid it — seeking higher ground, with one's belongings — or to try to control and protect against it? I know it is the former, not the latter. I understand the human tendency to not get involved in a mud wrestling. But at some point, I fear and suspect, such chronic hatred — even the silent tolerance of the mud-fest — weakens the foundation of the entire community. Weeds spread, hate spreads.

Or maybe not. Maybe there is only one scapegoat. Maybe it all begins and ends there. But I do not think so.

One year, not too long after our group formed, we got a big grant from Duke University's Indivisible Project, which selected twelve communities from around the country that were working on various issues involving social justice and democracy. The project brought in a professional photographer as well as an oral historian to document our stewardship forestry project and our community at this point in time — a historical reference point. The project then awarded us a $10,000 grant that could be used only on a community celebration: something to signify the end of the event.

We hired an internationally acclaimed puppeteer, Beth Nixon, to be an artist-in-residence in the Troy and Yaak schools, teaching them how to construct giant puppets and write, all on their own, a play — a pageant, a spectacle — using the puppets they made. Massive high-finned, long-tailed bright red dragons, spear-waving Kootenai Indians towering twenty feet above their bearers, borne on sophisticated constructs of harness belts and ingenious shoulder frames; a giant slug, glorious comets and mountains and suns and moons, a giant logger with giant ax and giant tree beside him, a thirty-foot-long aquamarine bewhiskered sturgeon (the eight sturdy legs transporting it below appearing as those of a centipede); angels, fairies, a three-part Yaak Ness Monster, and many more.

Beth worked seven days a week, sometimes twenty-four hours a day, shuttling between Troy and the Yaak, working individually with the 14 children in the one-room log cabin Yaak school (kindergarten through eighth grade) and the 227 children in Morrison Elementary and Troy Junior High.

Because the YVFC was sponsoring the project, however, a gang of eleven Yaak folks signed a letter of protest about it, attesting that the children's parents (and the larger community) were derelict in their duties for allowing this project to sneak into their community (underwritten by the wildly liberal Pew Charitable Trust, for heaven's sake!). The signatories (who had never discussed any of their lamentations with the Forest Council, or the school board, took particular pains to criticize one of the children's many creations, the Yaak Ness Monster — complaining, among other things, that it was fictional, not historical: that there was no such thing as a Yaak Ness Monster.

I want to tell you, some years, winters can get pretty long around here.

It never ends. Your hide gets thicker and thicker, and yet you have to remain sensate: you can't become an old leatherback turtle. The opposition, for lack of better words — or call it the matrix of suspicion and self-loathing, if you must — reached a new and breathtaking low this winter. (February and August are the months that seem to weigh heaviest upon their fevered minds; and are also, not coincidentally, in my view, the months of greatest alcohol and substance abuse — in February the sunlight's been gone the longest, and in August it's too stifling hot to even move.)

A year or two after the puppet protest, a letter appeared in the paper saying I seemed like a nice enough guy, but that my intent was to turn the entire million acres into one vast wilderness, outlaw the cutting of any tree seven inches in diameter or larger, and move all the humans (except, presumably, myself) out of the valley.

For column after column the attacker went on — a man who'd never uttered the first peep to me about forest management or bothered to ask my views, even though we'd gone for a walk together one day with a mutual friend, searching for a sign of an elk our friend thought he might have hit while out hunting.

This letter writer concluded by reiterating that although I was in essence a liar with secret agendas beneath even the lies (seven-inch logs only!), he still hoped my daughters would deliver the Girl Scout cookies he'd ordered from them earlier in the year.

We had a visit about that: myself and the letter writer, myself and the newspaper editor (who later came to denounce that particular year's campaign against the Yaak Valley Forest Council as "fascism"), and, finally, and painfully, myself and the girls. I would much rather they never know of such things, and don't discuss them when they're present; but this, of course, was different. I didn't want someone at school — much less in their Girl Scout troop — to be asking them what the heck was going on with the Girl Scout cookies. What might be funny to a crew of adults down at the bar might be a brand of humor too sophisticated and complex for a first- or fourth-grader.

I want to be clear that this is no longer how Lincoln

County is, and that I am chronicling, for the historical record, the old days. The reason we went forty-four years without wilderness.

As an activist, you've got to be perfect. You've got to be good. And maybe — no, certainly — this is one of the mixed blessings of my life, one of the greatest blessings in disguise.

Growing up in the pollution-cloaked suburbs of Houston, with toxic clouds of benzene wreathing our city like the rings around Saturn, I was comfortable. Even later, in the bohemian and hand-to-mouth existence of literature, and the hardscrabble scramble of the unemployed or self-employed freelance writer — scratching out book reviews, poems, essays, hunting and fishing articles, and teaching workshops — I was comfortable.

I don't think I took that comfort, or any of my blessings, for granted: the joy at having escaped the cityscape of Houston (and later, Jackson, Mississippi), the joy of the green world, the joy of the profoundly wild landscape in which every representative around in creation, since the time of the Ice Age, was still present. The joy, even if it was a challenge, of working for myself, of being my own boss. The joy of getting lost in a dream, while story writing, and in that tracking, that hunting, learning new truths about humanity and any manner of other things.

But there is an opportunity, also, in being the most hated man in the largest county in the United States.

It never bothered me at all, when I was young — and still does not, overmuch — to be physically uncomfortable. I would even seek out, and glory in, inclement weather, hiking all day regardless of thunderstorms, hundred-degree heat, or heavy snow or subzero cold. I had to get out, had to engage with the landscape in all seasons, had to learn every ridge and forest, and every animal. In my thrashings through alder and dense spruce and pine thickets, bears would run away before my clumsy advance, their spoor still steaming — glimpses of parts of the animal, or sometimes the entire animal itself, hurtling through the woods — while mountain lions, always more frightening, paused to look at me curiously with the insolence of the world's largest housecats, clearly wondering, *What would he taste like?*, clearly wondering, *What would it cost me to take him?*

I got lost on almost every outing — following no map in my mind or on paper and carrying no compass or travel plan, but merely following the land, and ending up, at dark and beyond, wherever I ended up.

Far wilder to me, however, was the terrain of humans, and the complex negotiations — the home range, to use a naturalist's term — within the relationships of the human community: friends, strangers, acquaintances. Craving and cherishing solitude, and then finding it, I almost surely would have written more stories, but I also almost surely would have gone further to seed, becoming an old-man Yaak hermit hiding out in the beautiful mountains. Rather than indulging that desire, I have increasingly sought out a wider cast of community.

Left to my own devices, and uninjured, I would never have attempted that gambit, would never have bartered or courted rejection. But rejected — fiercely, by those who I never even met — I was forced to reach out for human community and tenderness amid harshness. I would have missed out on that whole experience, other than the love of family. People like Robyn and her husband, Jimmy, and my dearest of friends, Tim and Joanne Linehan. The wisdom, humor, and passion of Rebecca Manna. Bill and Sue Jansson.

Without the relentless attacks and — in some ways, worse — the always simmering, always present atmosphere of hate — a paltry, puny air, such as a traveler might find on another planet (Mars, perhaps) — I would surely have never been forced, would never have dared to ask for or perhaps even to desire that other kind of air.

You've got to be perfect, in the fishbowl. I don't know how I haven't cracked. I guess the woods themselves — not just the pristine, unprotected backcountry but even the hard-used frontcountry tucked up against those last little wild gardens — absorb a lot of the toxicity, as do the marshes and meadows in spring, as do the gravelly rivers, as do the shapes of the hills; the sight of the mountains, the odors and sounds of the woods, and the gear work of the seasons.

I believe that probably this valley is a place for tearing down — for fire and rot and ice — but that perhaps someday, maybe a long time from now, or maybe not, it might be a place for healing too. It is not a coincidence, a stroke of luck, that everything's still hanging on here, that despite the harshness of all that's been thrown at this forest — nearly ten thousand miles of roads beribboning its mountains, carved and scribed into and around one mountain after another — nothing has gone extinct.

There is a spirit in the woods. With this, even my friends who prefer the structure of formal assembly in more orthodox houses of worship, following the ancient paths of scripture and teachings, would surely agree.

You desire anonymity, and non-hatred: you crave to be judged only on your actions of the day, not the rumors that cascade before you like a maelstrom of wind-riven, toppling timber, and which lie also behind you and around you in all. You want nothing more — no other identity — than to be your children's father, your wife's husband, and your friends' friend. A hard worker, dependable and honest. You want a few days — or a few years, or maybe even the rest of your life, already past the midpoint — in which you step out of the cage.

Step out anyway, don't pay any attention to them, a caring reader might say. *Ignore them, don't let the bastards get you down, just go about your business as if they don't exist.* But that would be false too, for they do exist, and in a small community they are paradoxically not small but as large and briefly significant — for the short remaining span of their own lives, anyway — as the weather itself, or the seasons. Windstorm, drought, gentle rain, sun. In a small community, within the town limits, they are the landscape, and I haven't figured out how to play it both ways: to ignore some and attend to others. Such a strategy doesn't have the ring of truth to it; it does not possess a biological integrity.

The longer the personal attacks go on, and the worse they become — all because you love the wild country passionately and are in some ways hostage to that love — the more desperately you want to achieve your goals so that there will be an end to it. You want wilderness in those fourteen roadless areas more intensely than ever — for their own sake, as always, but now for yours too — as if this and only this can validate or erase the decades of burden of being the scapegoat for the heart of darkness.

Friends from afar who see a hateful letter in the newspaper now and again will say, "Don't worry; it's fear, not hate" — but I disagree. It's plain old hate, with hatred's awful, whispering indulgences.

Not since the hate-blinded civil rights furies of the Deep South have I seen such unyielding, unthinking, uninformed, and elemental anger. It is not simply economic deprivation; it is plain old hate, allowed to flourish — tolerated, in either the silences or the winks, the looking the other way.

It's been twenty-one years, thus far, of almost nonstop hate. I look back now with amazement that it was ever any other way: a dim remembrance.

I know I should relax, and not fight the iron bars that surround me; that I should simply duck my head and proceed on, picking my way through that hailstorm of fallen timber, the crashing of psychic forest windstorm that seems to precede me. It is what it is, and this is my life. Contrary to earlier-held beliefs, perhaps we don't always get to choose our lives, or the way other people view us.

I need to reiterate: I am not the only one. There are so

many others now: more, thankfully, than can be named — though it is also true, unfortunately, that too many of the old bomb-throwers exist, renegade, destructive outliers in far-flung, scattered pockets, governed exclusively by fear, bitterness, and self-pity, and terrified of hope. Such outliers know, from long experience, how to despoil hope. It is all too easy, in a small town or a small rural community, to tear something down — and upon such tearing down, what politician would have the bravery, the courage, to then step in and do the right thing anyway, with so few votes at play, here in the outback, and surely with no campaign contributions to come from so impoverished a region?

I got roped into this gig through love — entered into it not knowing the consequences, and now simply don't know how to back out, don't know how to quit.

My own present situation, then, is and has been mainly one of endurance. Those of my friends, however — as they have seen the consequences of what they will be signing up for, and getting into — are those of courage.

It was no easier for people like Tony Johnson, who used to work at the Stimson mill before it went out of business, to stand up for wilderness, or for his wife, Cindy, who worked for the Forest Service: the very organization with which we often — particularly in the early days — found ourselves in conflict. Bill Janssen — a road builder by profession — certainly didn't need to put his neck out there and advocate for no more new roads, nor did his wife, Sue, who at the time we started was president of the school board.

The executive director of the Yaak Valley Forest Council,

Robyn, has almost single-handedly steered our organization toward being one that is as respected as a peacemaker as it is as a combatant. She has done this by hunting down our traditional adversaries within the Forest Service and the larger community, as well as any and all elected officials, and visiting with them one on one, again and again, trying to help dissipate their fears and dispel the ridiculous myths. Her message has been consistent — our group supports local loggers, and sustainable logging in the frontcountry; and we want wilderness protection for the roadless areas. And because of her cheerful demeanor and unflagging optimism — this tiny woman who when she started knew next to nothing about forestry issues but was eager to learn — she was not, and is not, perceived as a threat but instead as a potential partner, a potential ally.

She is making things work. She is making things in a small community work the way they are supposed to work. There are still a handful of self-pitying pissed-at-the-world malcontents — and always will be — who cannot help themselves, and who will always bother themselves with simply trying to tear things down rather than identifying common ground and working to achieve solutions. It has always been this way, to some extent, among some. But over the many years we have learned who these individuals are, and after decades of trying, we have finally learned not to invest hope or energy in those rabble-rousing few. The world, and the arc of the future, will pass them by — doubtless this is part of their fury — and already is passing them by.

In the meantime, there are so many people, an increasing

number of people, who are interested in listening to Robyn and to the goals and ideas of our group. Maybe agreeing, or maybe not, but for the first time, listening: which is the first and necessary step on the way to trust, and on the way to action and resolution. At last count, she sits on nine different committees or subcommittees within the county.

So overburdened is she, season by season and year by year, that while our board once joked nervously about keeping her happy and well rested, we now speak openly about Life After Robyn.

No one can keep going at this pace. We're just kind of pushing on, in an eternal redline howl — trying, where we can, to be proactive, but more often than not plugging the leaks and rifts springing in the earthen bulwarks of environmental protection.

Like the rest of us, Robyn didn't move up here for this — never dreamed she'd get drawn into it. Her husband, Jimmy, owns and operates Quality Solar, designing and installing and maintaining alternative energy systems in the area — a fact in which I find lovely metaphor. Robyn and Jimmy, like many of us, as I mentioned, live off the grid, procuring their power from nontraditional sources. When she and Jimmy moved to the Yaak, they built a small cabin in the valley between the Pink Mountain and Roderick Mountain roadless areas, along one of only two main roads in the Yaak, and sought — and still seek — a quiet life of reflection amid nature in each of its four powerful seasons up here. They sought, and still seek, invisibility and a silence within, rather than clamant discourse. They seek healing, want urgently and increasingly — even now, this late in life — to take from the landscape, to heal using that which this green valley has to yield to their spirits and souls, rather than to give, and give more. Robyn in particular desires to sit down in her garden in the morning sun and to do nothing more than dig in the dirt all day, not unlike the manner of the bears living in the mountains just beyond her.

Maybe next year. Maybe this year.

Tim Linehan's the only one who's been shot at — a bullet whistling past when he floated his boat down the Kootenai River one day — and he and his wife and business partner, Joanne, had some local business contracts canceled as well as a result of their commitment to a moderate solution for Yaak wilderness. Ironically, their economic development and well-being — which is to say, in part, the county's economic development and well-being — would, or should, be enhanced by wilderness protection for some of these last few roadless areas, wilderness being the gold standard of such designations and possessing a value-added cachet that would find favor with their potential bed-and-breakfast and sporting clients. In a phrase well known to the economies fortunate enough to have such designations, wilderness is good for business.

Tim's an utter gentleman (he's been named the Montana Guide of the Year on multiple occasions), and even when folks freak out and criticize him, he continues trying to maintain relationships with them, explaining his position while listening diplomatically to theirs. And Joanne, likewise, is an utter gentlewoman. Their talents and contributions are peaceful. In a time of war, this can be one of the greatest of blessings.

Another great piece of luck we've had involves our youngest employee, Sarah Canepa, who was born and raised here in Lincoln County. She graduated from Troy High School as valedictorian, went off to study forestry at the University of Montana, joined the Peace Corps, and now, in her first "real" job, is the Forest Watch coordinator for the YVFC. It's kind of an amazing thing, when you think about it: how she was just a little kid when the rest of us started out on this dream, and now here she is, commenting on proposed timber sales and forest policies for us, and taking our dream, our hopes, deep into the next century. It's strange, and it's awesome.

About our first executive director, Scott Daily, there are easily a hundred great stories, but there's one I want to share not because of its uniqueness but its commonality.

Scott and his girlfriend (now his wife), Sherrie, showed up here, in May of '97 — children, really, in their early twenties. They had driven nonstop from Pennsylvania, to arrive in the valley to hear the Orion Society's Forgotten Language Tour — Terry Tempest Williams, Robert Michael Pyle, Richard Nelson, and Janisse Ray — read stories and essays in various small towns throughout Lincoln County.

A spring microburst had torn through the region that afternoon and evening, with localized winds in excess of two hundred miles an hour, howling and slashing with knives of hail and lightning, knocking out the power for hundreds of miles in all directions. Roads were impassable for hours.

Stranded motorists everywhere were busy trying to gnaw their way out of nearly impossible grids and mazes of the wind-felled trees that latticed all roads like a massive game of jackstraw pick-up sticks. With the ubiquitous crosscut saws, handsaws, chain saws, axes, and hatchets that travelers always carry in their cars and trucks, the motorists were one by one engaged in the group-solidarity act of trying to carve their way back into the conjoined stream of all the others — laboring to link back up. And after the storm had finally passed (the river whitecaps cresting ten and twelve feet, and leaning in the other direction, so that the river's course appeared to have reversed) and everyone had limped back home (our vehicles dinged and battered by the ferocious hail, which still lined the roads and streets thick with slush, and the air ripe and sweet with the Christmas tree odor of new-sawn wood and crushed green boughs) — after all that (with every gas station shut down for lack of electricity, and candles in every window, in the long-gathering dim twilight of summer dusk), Scott came limping into town like some rough beast, wild-eyed and dazed after having driven twenty-four hours to get here, to the last reading, and arriving, dammit, an hour too late, delayed by the storm.

Such disynchrony, such roughness of passage, is, I think, one of the novitiate's rites of acceptance, one of the journey's many gates to this hard and farther land. It speaks to the Yaakness of the place — the way things will never turn out the way a traveler or a resident planned or envisioned — and in some ways, that preliminary rejection declares to me, more than any embrace or acceptance, that Scott and

Sherrie do belong; that such rejection, such challenge, is perhaps merely the valley's way of welcoming and testing those whom it desires most of all.

I know of no one up here who has not been crucible-forged — taken in, cast out, taken in, then rejected again, having to fight his or her way back at least twice before finally settling in to a kind of dynamic equilibrium, a biological and emotional fit to this farther blue land of spruce and snow, ice and rain and mist. It's always been a hard place to make a living — even the Kootenai people, by most accounts, didn't live up here year-round, preferring to locate their fish-based culture downvalley, near the confluence of the Yaak and the Kootenai, and instead only traveled up into the upper Yaak on hunting trips in the summer and fall (where they found, in the amazing old-growth forest, woodland caribou, and mountain goats up in the icy crags of the Little Ice Age). In this regard, the Yaak is a remarkably new land, differing even from its sister mountain range, the Cabinets, lying just to the south — within plain view — on the other side of the Kootenai River.

I keep coming back, again and again, to the story — or the most recent story — of the Yaak's creation, of how things got to be the way they are. I keep telling that story again and again, rolling it over and over in my mind, hoping that some answer, some clue for the future, can be found there, and some message, beyond the obvious one of patience. I keep thinking of the way the last ice sheet thinned rapidly in this area, helping to carve the bow of the Kootenai River, which comes down out of Canada in a big belly arc, taking in Libby and Troy before turning north again and traveling back up into Canada. (The word Yaak is thought to be the Kootenai word for arrow — the Yaak River charging hard, straight down out of the valley, resembling in that manner a straight-spined arrow fitted into the bow of the Kootenai.)

During the retreat of the last glaciers, while the Cabinets were stealing the show — grinding, rearing, shouting, creaking, rasping, squeaking amid the thinning islands of going-away ice — the Yaak country, as I've mentioned, lay sleeping beneath several thousand feet of blue ice, like some mythic princess. Only in the very highest portions of the Yaak — Mount Henry, Northwest Peaks, Roderick country, Buckhorn Ridge, and a few other of the highest islands of uplifted stone — was it glaciated, at its very tips; elsewhere, all remained sleeping, compressed beneath a mile or more of ice, even as just across the river the other mountains were being exposed, borne back into the bright light of day and the cold visages of starlight.

While the Cabinets were being fitted for the sky, the Yaak was undergoing that more secret, entirely invisible transformation, with the border and foundations of the Yaak's own internal cathedrals and civilizations being formed and fitted, though not yet revealed to the world.

No ice can last forever, and when even that mile of diamond-dense blue ice finally melted, it was an entirely different landscape that was presented to the world. The shapes of the Yaak were softer, more gentle, supercompressed but not broken or fractured — pressed and molded instead into the pleasing, soothing, calming shapes of muscles, and even the forms of animals, some recumbent and still sleeping, with others appearing to be upright and walking: bears, otters, lions, wolves, wolverines. The flank of an elk, the hump of a trout, the shoulder of a man, the figure of a woman, sleeping, then just awakening, rising up on one elbow to look around at the world this time.

I do not suppose that that mood, that spirit, will last forever in the Yaak, still so new in the world. But to anyone beholding the shape of those last uncut, unaltered hills, and the simple yet elegant curves of its creation, there is a magic, and a softening within, that is restorative to the troubled or jagged places within the viewer. The sight of the Yaak — or rather, the unbroken Yaak — soothes and heals.

That said — and there is no one who has visited or glimpsed the Yaak who does not know what I am speaking of — there is obviously an enormous power in the landscape, understated, as if sometimes even still just beneath the surface, so recently has the ice gone away. (And a power too, I think, in that nothing else but the ice has gone away. Everything else — grizzlies, moonworts, wolves, goshawks, all of it, the entire creation — still exists here, with invisible lines of grace, and invisible lines of connection, laced throughout the forest, grizzly to wolf, grouse to aspen, swallowtail to cloud drift, forest fire to mushroom, in ways we once knew but rarely now experience.)

There's an immediately felt and yet immeasurable power in these connections — and while it is one thing to stand briefly in the presence of such power, it is quite another thing to wade into the center of such a force, even such a healing force, and presume to set up camp and live amid it.

Again and again, the valley seeks to push out those who enter. It's an almost impossible place to make a living — there is no one who could not be making more money doing what they do somewhere else — but the valley presses and shapes and sculpts the individual, almost from the very beginning, in other ways too.

And for a while, you complain and fight it, this change. You glory in the healing and fret about the setbacks, and the tearing down.

You will not become sharper-edged in the Yaak. You will not be lifted up to the bright sky with sharpened, gleaming ridges.

You descend, as if into a place of sleep. Steadily, slowly, ceaselessly, you are remade. You disappear. You are absorbed.

All this to say, Scott was as jagged-edged as they come when he and Sherrie came sailing in that stormy night eleven years ago. Earnest and passionate and excitable, he spent a lot of time trying to talk to folks in the bars about his need for wilderness, and got in a lot of fistfights during that time. A rabid tree-hugger, he had his car firebombed and was vilified almost as regularly as I was.

Scott fell from a ladder a couple of years ago, broke his jaw and shoulder; the metaphor may seem simple, that he overextended. But he also healed up. He's fine now.

He moves more carefully these days. He still goes down to

the bars, hangs out and listens to music and likes to visit. But he listens a lot now. As if we are all finally beginning to realize we might yet still be moving around beneath thousands of feet of blue ice.

Which is, I think, what all of us up here wish and desire: a pace and rhythm and a way of being in the world with which we are comfortable.

The old world was so fast, from what little I remember of it, the ice of those retreating glaciers thinning so rapidly in the Cabinets as to seem to be galloping away.

We're still learning to adjust our pace up here in the Yaak. We're still not quite fitted to the landscape. But we're trying, or are learning to try.

Still, I wish we'd hurry up and get the wilderness protected while it's still there. That's the only part we haven't figured out how to back off of. That desire is the only part that seems to have been sleeping under the ice long enough.

11

Bear Spray Stories

Every time I get sprayed, I have to laugh. It's like, *how dumb can I get?* But each time it happens, I tell myself it won't happen again, that there's no way I'll make that mistake twice.

I have been sprayed far more times than any bear I know of. I think something's backwards here. In fact, I don't know that a grizzly bear's ever been sprayed in the Cabinet-Yaak ecosystem. They are so exquisitely rare, so imminently imperiled, that one's immediate response upon seeing one, on the most infrequent of occasions, should not be to discharge hot pepper spray at it but to marvel in heartfelt awe at one's luck in catching such a glimpse.

To even come across the tracks of a grizzly, up in this last corner of wilderness, last corner of history, is a spectacular event.

Perhaps I keep spraying myself with pepper spray out of some subconscious effort to harm myself, so troubled am I by the implicit disrespect, or even antagonism, of the act: carrying a loaded weapon into the territory of a shy, endangered creature who, if not necessarily a friend, is certainly no enemy.

The guardian of the forest: the guardian of wild places.

My first experience with being sprayed happened way back in college, in northern Utah. I was sitting in a late-night diner on a date with a Mormon girl, and we were about to pay for our meals and leave. Her purse was open — she had gone to the restroom — and in the top of it was a tiny aerosol spray can of what I took to be breath freshener. Having just finished off a plate of corned beef hash, and anticipating perhaps the evening ahead, I picked up the little spray can and squirted a stream from it into my mouth: expecting mint, or peppermint. Expecting romance.

What I got instead was the rough equivalent of a mule kick to the face. I fell backwards off my stool, shouting and retching as a kaleidoscope of pain blossomed, gold-starred, across my palate. A most memorable sight it must have been for my date when, returning from the restroom, she found her companion spinning clockwise on the floor, his corned beef hash spilled out in front of him, and clawing at his face. It felt as if my face were on fire, and I wished for nothing less than a miracle, that someone would pour a bucket of cold water over me.

Somehow I got to my feet and bulled my way blindly, careening against horrified onlookers, to the men's room, where I shoved my head into a sink and began dousing the flames. It was some time before the pain subsided enough for me to come back down to earth, and rest assured that when I came back out into the diner my date was gone.

I used to move through these woods up here like the wind, with no forethought of consequence or danger, sliding instead along the contours, bending this way and that through the bottoms of dark-night ravines without a flashlight and galloping headlong atop windy ridges, unconcerned about anything, least of all bears. In twenty-one years of hiking these sawed-over hills, I've seen twelve grizzlies, and half of them have fled from me as if believing my sole intent in life, the reason I was in their woods, was to get them, while the other six merely sat down and studied me, sniffing the air with deeply troubled expressions, as if thinking, *Well, there goes the neighborhood.*

In all cases, I turned around and left the heart of their territory a little embarrassed at having intruded on so great and private a creature.

I'm not sure at what point I decided to begin carrying the clunky holster of spray, nor am I even sure for what reason. There had always been rare and certain mornings when before embarking on a hike into wild country, I'd get a brief feeling of uneasiness, and would on those days enter the woods with more caution, more respect, rather than with the euphoria, the unthinking exuberance of the past. But I'd had no truly life-threatening encounters. Lions had stalked me before, and a black bear had charged me — but the grizzlies, for whom the spray was designed and marketed, never. In addition to being cumbersome, the cans were expensive as hell, and seemed like nothing more than a shortcut to irresponsibility.

But as anyone who's a parent can attest, you slow down once you have children. You become deeply aware of how important it is to them that you stick around. Past extravagances seem extraordinarily foolish.

I bought one of the spray cans, and on those days when I felt a bit of tension in the valley, or would be passing through or near places where I knew there were bears, I carried it. On my hip, it felt like a small fire extinguisher, and again, moving with it through the country of bears, I would often find myself feeling embarrassed, as if I had somehow betrayed them, or betrayed some implicit trust, some cautious understanding.

But it wasn't just for my family that I carried the spray into the woods now, on certain days, certain trips. It was, I told myself, for the bears themselves: to protect them from my own blunders and mistakes, should I be foolish or careless enough to wander into a situation that forced one of them to respond with aggression.

If a bear charged me, attacked me, injured me, it would be bad for that bear not from my own hand, but from the fears of others, who would say, *We told you the woods were dangerous;* and bad, then, for all bears, as in our species' unimaginative way we extrapolated immediately, totally, the justified actions of one to serve as the unjustified intent of all, and of perhaps also the intent of the dark harbor of the wilderness itself — humans taking that one small and specific incident, a bear charge, and translating it onto the great abstract canvas of All, with our brutal penchant, our instinct, for stereotyping.

And think of this too, I tell myself: what better lesson to deliver to a bear that might find itself cornered into a position where it feels it must charge, than to receive a healthy dose, a snootful, of liquefied capsicum powder? Imagine the tremblings, the terror in that animal's poor heart, the next time and every time thereafter it scented a human entering its woods? Perhaps, by spraying the right bear at the right time, I might actually save that bear. Perhaps, by such a defense, even the wild woods themselves might be saved; though even as I suggest these hypotheses to myself, I am aware of the vast faults in logic beneath them — as if I am crossing a sheet of crackling, soggy ice.

I think I carry the spray on certain days mostly because, for a number of reasons, I do not care to be killed and eaten, despite the romantic notion of the bear then taking my heart into his or hers: a rough and inefficient though gloriously sublime transfer of calories. (As an activist who's spent many years laboring on behalf of the roadless landscapes, the public wildlands, which grizzlies and other wild things need desperately to survive, it has not gone unconsidered by me the humor, even delight, representatives of the various extractive industries seeking to liquidate those last wildlands would find in the irony of my being consumed by one of the things I professed to seek to defend; and from that awareness too I am careful, aware of nature's love of irony, fit, and counterbalance . . .)

The second time I was sprayed was actually the first time I caught a dose of one of the big cans of bear spray. It was summertime, and I was out picking huckleberries with my young daughters. I'd seen bear scat in the area, but that wasn't unusual; you can't not find bear scat in a huckleberry field, and because of the patch's proximity to a road, I figured it was probably the sign of a black bear — knowing that the grizzlies prefer, for the most part, the deeper, wilder interiors of the forest, as far away from the activities of man as possible.

Further, we scheduled our berry-picking during the heat of the day, when the bears, with their heavy coats, would be less likely to be out and about.

Still, I carried my spray; and because the bushes were high and we were sitting beneath them, swathed in leafy green light, our voices muffled as we plucked the sweet purple berries, I kept the holster open and had the orange safety valve already popped off, so that I could use the spray immediately, if necessary. I kept the girls close to me — no more than ten paces away at any time.

We had been picking for almost an hour and had fallen into that silent, peaceful, autumnal trance of the hunter-gatherer, when, on a steep hillside, I shifted my weight and, in crouching down, squeezed the trigger in the fold formed between my stomach and thigh.

I felt and heard a thunderous, intestinal gurgling down in that vicinity — a hissing sound as loud as if a tire had been gashed — and a moment later a red mushroom cloud of pepper vapor erupted from beneath the denim of my overalls, and my thigh began to burn as if wasp-stung. I shot straight up, yowling, and by my standing up the trigger mechanism was released so that the spray stopped.

That one wasn't so bad. The emission was localized, leaving a red spot roughly the size of a silver dollar atop my thigh, safely distanced from any tender membranes — though all in all, a close call.

The third time I was sprayed, it was my dog who got me, though still and again, as always, it was I who was responsible.

The berry season was over, and Point and I had been out hunting grouse that afternoon, and I'd stopped off at the tavern briefly before heading home. It was dark by that time, and Point was riding up front with me, as he always does. I guess he was hungry or something, because he hopped into the cab section of the truck and began nosing around in there. (Perhaps he was attracted to the scent of red pepper, as even the bears themselves are said to be drawn sometimes by curiosity.)

I don't know if I had left the safety valve off, or if Point dislodged it with his scrabbling. In any event, once again I heard that telltale squirting, spraying sound and the cab of the truck was filled immediately with a cloud of red pepper. I barely had time to pull over to the side of the road before being overcome with stinging blindness and an involuntary, spasmodic attack of dry heaves.

With the truck parked crookedly, driven half into the bushes, I bailed out of the cab as if fleeing a burning structure, and wobbled sightlessly in circles, coughing and gagging, hissing thin trickles of mad-dog drool and trying to spit up, though nothing was in me to come out.

A neighbor came driving down the dark road, driving slowly — paused, evaluating the strange scene in his headlights — and then (doubtless shaking his head and clucking, believing I'd had a few too many at the saloon) eased on past, not wanting to intrude on my evident misery. There was a creek down in the woods below. I hurried toward it in the darkness, pawing at my eyes and colliding with trees, crashing over saplings, my dog stumbling behind me, and we threw ourselves down into the cool, shallow water and splashed it onto our faces.

It was becoming slowly evident to me that it was not really the bears I had to worry about.

The fourth time was really a corker. My wife and I decided to take the girls on one last summer picnic in the final week of August before school started back up. The place I wanted to take them was a beautiful waterfall that could be reached after a long hike along the river through beautiful old-growth larch trees. It was also true that a year before, in that same drainage, a large male grizzly, one with whom the biologists were familiar and who weighed, they said, more than six hundred pounds, had bluff-charged a bow hunter who had stumbled onto him in some brush from downwind as the bear was napping.

The cruising range for such a creature in these parts is probably around five hundred square miles. And he was a good bear, a great bear: even in his summer ire, he'd only bluffed. There were more fistfights down at the bar that summer, more murders down in the little town of Kalispell, more lightning strikes, more *anything*, than there were bear problems in this valley that year.

But still, I carried the spray. Again.

It was a lovely day for a hike: hot as an iron out in the open, but cooler beneath the canopy of the old forest.

Passing through a marshy glen of alder, we found the fresh tracks of moose and bear — grizzly, big grizzly.

I took the safety cap off my canister, and we proceeded, talking loudly.

Of course we did not see a bear (or a moose, or even a deer, talking as we were). But I did spray myself again, when I knelt down to retie a boot lace.

I was wearing overalls, and this time the pepper spray mushroomed up inside me, a balloon of pain that had its unfortunate epicenter in a region that was pretty much midgroin.

Once more I hit the river, but so saturated was my skin that I couldn't get it all scrubbed off. My overalls were saturated too, and my underpants were totaled, trashed, a dripping red wad of pepper spray. I had to take them off and stuff them into my backpack.

I rinsed my overalls in the river and was able to make the rest of the hike in a hunched-over limp — though any time the denim brushed against me, fore or aft, it set off a new surge of pain.

I couldn't just walk back home naked, in nothing but my hiking boots. So while the girls swam and picnicked, I gathered lichen and moss from the old forest and began stuffing them into my overalls, like padding — big fistfuls of the black lichen, *Bryoria,* also called old-man's beard — which formed a cushion between my fire-stained overalls and my tender pale skin.

By the time I had my clothes stuffed enough so that no denim was touching me, it looked as if I too could have weighed six hundred pounds. Curls of black lichen protruded from the neck of my shirt and from beneath the sleeves of my T-shirt. Wisps of black tuft gathered around the tops of my boots on the walk home, and as I lurched humpbacked through the forest, pausing from time to time to readjust the shifting lichen, I'm sure I looked like nothing less than a werewolf, and it was both alarming and touching at how matter-of-factly my daughters accepted this strangeness. I often wonder what random images from childhood my girls will take with them to remember as adults, and as I hobbled along behind them that bright sunny day, stopping occasionally to pull down a new bundle of moss before stuffing it into my overalls, I had the sinking feeling that this might be one of those memories, those indelible images.

One of the fine things about living in the woods is that you often (and quickly) forget how you might appear to the outside world — a forgetfulness that is proportionate, of course, to the reduction of your involvement with that world. Among your neighbors, there's no need to try to represent yourself as being something or someone you're not; to do so, in fact, would be ridiculous — like wearing a Halloween mask to supper one evening. For better or worse, in a small community, we know pretty intimately one another's strengths and limitations.

What I mean to be saying is that by the time we stopped for gas at the mercantile on our way home, I had forgotten that I was stuffed with about four hundred cubic centimeters of lichen. In fact, it was kind of comfortable. When I walked in to pay for the gas, however, I was reminded of it when Keith informed me, with some concern, that my fly was open.

Indeed it was, and sticking out from behind the overalls' buttons was a leaking mass of lichen. I pulled it free — there was a long spool of it in there — and thanked him, paid for my gas, and left. We respect one another's privacy up here.

Spraying myself with my bear spray — hosing myself down with it — is minor-league stuff — though evidence enough of an increasing clumsiness, a distraction, that may or may not be an appropriate way to enter bear country. (Part of me wants to caution myself, *Wake up!;* though at the same time another part of me wants to say, *What are the woods for, if not a place to dream?*)

The last really, really dumb thing I ever did was back when Elizabeth was pregnant with our first daughter, Mary Katherine. I was crossing a frozen river on snowshoes, at dusk, in February, when I went through the ice.

The water, however, was only knee-deep in that one stretch, though I didn't know it at the time.

I stood there in the gathering darkness, up to my knees in rushing cold water, and I thought, *Okay, my life must change. Wake up.*

We need every last bit of big wild country kept wild, for bears and other wild things. We need wild country for young people to be young in, and for older people to look at and remember, and, if they are still willing, to continue to enter it, with respect, caution — honoring quietness, honoring privacy, always mindful of the consequences of one's actions, and one's responsibilities as well as one's rights.

I carry the spray with me sometimes now not as protection against the bear's or the lion's ferocity, but against my own foolishness. Someday I hope to be too old to be able to walk all over this valley, and when I am, I hope that there are still grizzly bears, wild grizzly bears, young grizzly bears, living as they have always lived, in those last far corners where we have not yet built roads or dams or mines.

The bears are not the danger; the wilderness is not the danger; nature is not the danger. We are the danger, and a world without these things, or with these things diminished — bears, wilderness, wild nature — is not a place I care to dwell. I am clumsy in that world as well. It is not nature's fault that I stumble. It is in wild nature that I most feel such stumbling is all right — approaching with my clumsiness sometimes even a prayerful kind of grace, and laughing and marveling at the richness of a wilder, farther world that for the most part still lies beyond our touch, our reach, and even our understanding. We cannot really protect ourselves against such wonder. We can only protect ourselves against the vices of inattention and disrespect.

We need more big wild country against which to be wonderfully, foolishly human while the rest of the animal world looks on, and perhaps marvels.

12

Rebecca's "My Hair Is on Fire" Lobster Soup

THE SENATOR'S OFFICE is aflame. My friends and I are having lunch with his senior policy advisor, Rebecca Manna, petitioning her and the senator to support an economic development package for north Lincoln County that will include greater assistance for the last remaining roadless areas in the Yaak — wilderness, in the Land the Wilderness Act Forgot, way back in 1964 — as well as technological upgrades for our rural schools (digital broadband capabilities and long-distance Cable in the Classroom), local highway beautification projects, revitalization of an ailing independent sawmill in Eureka, and increased funding for rural firefighters, particularly in the wildland-urban interface, for which, I suppose, the senator's very office might qualify at this very moment.

A poof and *pop!* of heated blue air soars past my nose,

scorches my eyebrows, singes the top of my hair, and then falls back to a wavering, wobbly orange flame that encases the leaking old Coleman stove, melting the counter in the senator's conference room only a little.

The policy director's desk is piled high with thousands of papers and letters, all of the utmost urgency and importance — we recognize and appreciate the rarity of an audience with her, and we are determined to make the most of it, hence our offer to prepare lunch in her office rather than traveling out somewhere, ordering cardboard pizza.

The senator and his staff have been good to the residents of Lincoln County, and we are hesitant to ask for one more snuffle at the trough, even though Troy and Eureka have traditionally been severely underserved, with the county seat, Libby, receiving most of the economic assistance.

Neither are we asking, in this instance, for straight pork — back before the war, in the Clinton years, we easily could have nibbled a bit from the massive budget surplus, but now those days are long gone — but are instead suggesting a work-incentive proposal, girded by alterations to tax code and stewardship forestry authorizations, wherein we might assemble a community forest (on private, not public land). The plan calls for the purchase and/or lease of a network of cutover industrial timberlands in Lincoln County, designing a system that will protect endangered species' habitat and preserve critical open space and traditional community access while providing (and preserving) an additional stream of fiber for area mills. Perhaps a co-op of western Montana mills could market materials produced and milled from the community forest as "wilderness wood." Revenues from this community forest can then help further fund the ailing budgets of our underserved rural schools.

Oh yeah, and we want a rifle range, new sidewalks (which is to say, our first sidewalks, where always before there have only been mud embankments), a swimming pool, snow-grooming equipment for the local snowmobile club as well as the local ski hill, and reauthorization of funding for our sheriff's department to help patrol the U.S.–Canada drug trafficking: and more.

So many ideas, and all for these piddling little fourteen roadless areas in the Yaak, the last 180,000 acres of roadless land, in a land historically shorted and always bartered away, poker-chipped out, in the rare Montana wilderness bills of the past. We are seeking a hero, a champion for the Yaak, and somewhere along the line — made half goofy, perhaps, by that siege mentality and fatigue of hope/no hope — we have gotten it into our minds that if we could only cook the perfect meal, or even the single, most perfect dish, the senator's heart would open further to understand even more clearly the depths of our love for these last roadless lands, and our desire to end this saga and go home to quiet lives, and that the senator, indeed the entire delegation, could then understand the incredible moderation of our ask: asking for the last of the last in a land where we have never gotten anything: not one single acre of wilderness has ever been designated north of the Kootenai River.

In meeting after meeting, and nurturing, in the most literal sense, our champion, we put forth our best efforts, trying to articulate, to transfer, the beauty of our beloved wildlands directly to the policy director. Northwest Peaks, Roderick and Grizzly and Pink mountains; Mount Henry, the West Fork, Buckhorn Ridge, and all our other little gardens of wildness: all beloved, and all rare.

It's astonishing to us, on these forays into politico-land, to see the other issues at play, and the relative puniness of our desires compared to the larger needs of the nation. First and foremost always, in Lincoln County — understandably — asbestos legislation must be passed to help treat the victims of W. R. Grace's toxic legacy (the membership of which spans all political groups, all religious beliefs; all community members are affected), the treatment of which can easily cost $500,000 per patient. We're always careful to explain that we never want any of our conservation or economic development proposals to displace or move ahead of, or jeopardize in any other way, that critical need.

But there are so many other national and international issues also seeming to originate here in Lincoln County: international water law via Canada's Lake Koocanusa and the Kootenai River, endangered species legislation, World Trade Organization softwood lumber tariffs, Social Security reform, Medicare and Medicaid legislation, Forest Service firefighting budgets, FAA, DOT, DEA, Border Patrol, Homeland Security concerns . . . For a county of only 19,000 residents, and the Yaak, a valley of only about 150 people — a valley of hermits — it sometimes occurs to me that we haven't perhaps picked the best spot after all from which to hold the rest of the world at bay; that indeed, so often, the borderlands of Lincoln County seem to be some psychic landscape, the source of so many of the difficult issues of the times.

And as a result of working this turf, Rebecca's hair almost always seems to be on fire, though she never complains, and she continues about her tasks seemingly uninterrupted by the flames: indeed, seeming sometimes to be fueled or nurtured by them, moving from one crisis to the next with firmness and resolve. Our own needs are so small compared to the world's, but they are felt passionately. And in their minuteness, are they not then easily and imminently attainable?

The language of wilderness in the Yaak — of wilderness to come — is that of loon, willow, black bear, wolverine, grizzly, feldspar, glacier, lupine. The language of our crude articulation, our cuisine and cookery, contains phrases like "clarify the butter" and "prepare a mirepoix" and "assemble the bouquet garni."

The language of our relationships with the sawmills contains phrases like "sustainable and predictable supply of small-diameter logs" and "market share" and "postburn value deterioration."

The language of our time spent in the senator's office contains phrases like "walk me around the mulberry bush" and "at the end of the day" and "provide drive-blocking." We speak of putting the ball across the goal line, and of the need for collaboration, and yet of the need also for sharp elbows.

The language of our relationships with the Forest Service

contains phrases like "purpose and need" and "historic range of variability" and "new incentives for collaborative and community stakeholder partnerships."

The language of our relationships with the business leaders in Lincoln County is that of "equity refuge" and "vertically integrated value-added product diversification" and "producer services."

So many dialects, so many tongues! Maybe we are not so crazed after all to think that one meal — one sweet meal, one perfect dish — can get us, finally, up and over that wall in this, the forty-fourth year and counting. That the perfect melt-in-your-mouth bite of the perfect meal can still, even now, bring together all participants, including past combatants, into one focused moment of mutual understanding in which the clarity of a solution is attained — an understanding and agreement that has been forty-four years in the aging, leading finally to the belated arrival of that understanding ultimately as intangible and immeasurable as might be the powerful undefined qualities and characteristics of taste. And somehow, we have gotten it into our minds that the solution, *wilderness in the Yaak,* will be as permanent and enduring as is the pleasure of the palate fading even in the moment, temporal and fleeting. We believe it.

The best meal of all, and the best recipe? A piece of French bread and thick yellow cheese, and a canteen of cold well water, on top of a nameless ridge in the Yaak, while looking down into the uncut basin below, in the autumn, with forests of larch stretching unbroken to the horizon. But in the meantime, this recipe, from the day Rebecca's office caught on fire. And if this doesn't work, then something else — some other ingredient. We'll never give up, or compromise our values, but we are getting long in the tooth, and we long desperately to have our lives back: to return to our gardens and kitchens, our poetry and our families.

Maybe this will finally be the year of the Yaak. Maybe this year.

GORDON HAMERSLEY'S LOBSTER, FENNEL, AND ORANGE SOUP

Gordon's Note: Serve this soup with some toasted baguette slices. Better yet, slather those baguette toasts with some garlicky aioli.

Cribbed almost directly from Gordon Hamersley's (with Joanne McAllister Smart) most excellent *Bistro Cooking at Home* (Broadway Books, 2003), with only slight modifications in the cooking and letter-writing process. Gordon is a Yaak Valley Forest Council supporter, and the owner of a wonderful restaurant in Boston, Hamersley's Bistro.

2 Lobsters, about 1½ pounds each
½ cup Pernod
Kosher salt
1 cup fresh orange juice (from about 2 oranges)
3 tablespoons olive oil
2 fennel bulbs, top stalks and any tough outer layers removed, cut into a small dice

2 teaspoons dried tarragon
Pinch of red pepper flakes
1 onion, chopped
Freshly ground black pepper
2 garlic cloves, chopped
½ tablespoon unsalted butter
3 medium tomatoes, quartered, or 2 cups chopped canned tomatoes
1 orange, skin and pith removed and cut into sections
1 tablespoon tomato paste
2 teaspoons chopped fresh tarragon
1 cup vermouth

FOR THE BROTH

In a pot large enough to hold the lobsters, bring about 6 quarts water to boil. Boot up computer in preparation for writing the Montana delegation — Senators Baucus and Tester, Representative Rehberg, and Governor Schweitzer, with a copy of your letter going also to the Yaak Valley Forest Council. Add the lobsters and about a teaspoon of salt. Bring the water back to a boil and cook the lobsters for five minutes. (You are not trying to cook the lobsters completely here; the meat will finish cooking when added to the hot soup.) Remove the lobsters from the pot and let them cool on a sided dish or sheet pan. Reserve 3 quarts of the lobster cooking water.

WHEN you can handle the lobsters, twist off the tails and claws from each and reserve them on the sided dish. Rinse the bodies under cold running water and reserve them separately. Remove the lobster meat from the tails and the claws.

Do this work over a bowl or sided baking sheet to collect the juices. Reserve the lobster meat, well covered, in the fridge, for up to 1 day.

HEAT the olive oil in a large soup pot over high heat. Put the lobster bodies in the pot and cook, stirring occasionally, for about 5 minutes. Reduce the heat to medium-high and add half of the fennel, the onion, garlic, tomatoes, and tomato paste. Continue to cook, stirring, for another 10 minutes. The lobster shells will darken and the mixture will become drier.

ADD the vermouth and Pernod to the pan. Bring to a boil over high heat, being alert to the chance that, like the director's hair on any given day, the Pernod too can ignite. (This is actually a good thing, as the slight char on the lobster bodies adds flavor; if the pan does flame, simply allow the flames to die down.) Let the Pernod boil away for a minute or two, stirring occasionally, and scraping up any bits stuck to the pan. Add the reserved lobster cooking water, orange juice, dried tarragon, and red pepper flakes. Also add any liquid that was collected while cutting up the lobster and gathering the meat. (Strain the liquid into the pot if there is sediment or bits of shell in it.) Bring to a boil over high heat, lower to a simmer, and cook the soup for 45 minutes.

REMOVE the lobster bodies from the pot — lifting them head up so that any liquid in the body cavity will drain back into the broth — and discard. Strain the broth into a clean pot, pressing down on the solids to squeeze out any liquid and flavor. Add more salt, and black pepper to taste. (This broth, which makes about 2 quarts, can be made a day ahead.)

TO SERVE

Heat the butter in a small sauté pan over medium-high heat until hot. Add the remaining fennel and cook until the fennel is tender, about 10 minutes. Add the orange sections and fresh tarragon and remove from the heat. Cut the lobster meat into small pieces and add it to the fennel mixture. Add the fennel, lobster, and orange mixture to the hot broth and allow the flavor to combine over medium heat for a few minutes before serving. Pass wilderness legislation subsequently.

Surely the way to effect the most lasting and durable change is to address as diverse a representation of the senses as possible: not only the heart, through our innate love of or connection to nature, and the mind, through a realization of the economic and social benefits of protecting the land, but the sense of taste as well. Pleasure is pleasure, whether intellectual, spiritual, or gustatory. We're hoping that all our pleasures will converge soon, in the Yaak.

13

Threshold

IT'S BEEN TWENTY-ONE YEARS, and we — the Yaak Valley Forest Council, and our desires to designate some wilderness in the Yaak — have never been closer. We're so close that we might already have passed the threshold and don't even realize it yet. For sure, the wilderness has not been protected yet, but just as surely, something has happened, something different and tenuous and beautiful, even if I do not know the name for it.

After decades of failure — of hearing how the majority of Lincoln County was afraid of wilderness — we decided to go out one more time and meet with opponents of wilderness and ask what they *did* want. We listened. We told our traditional opponents to make no mistake about it, we ourselves wanted wilderness, and that further, we understood that they were afraid that wilderness could be like a wildfire, or a contagion; or that by giving people a little taste of how wonderful it was, people might decide they wanted more and more of it: a thought that frightened, and still frightens, some folks up here. (The idea is surprisingly pervasive — the notion that once wilderness advocates "get their foot in the door" there'll be no stopping them. No stopping us. That *all* public lands will be folded into the National Wilderness Preservation System, and then all private lands, and after that, for good measure, the government will round up folks' guns, toss them in a big pit, and melt them down to make shackles with which to incarcerate their once free owners.)

Never mind that our real access to the forest is draining away — not through wilderness designation, but draining instead as if through ten thousand terrible gashes, as private or quasi-private lands owned by the big industrial timber companies are now being sold off in tiny lots, after the corporations cut all the timber off those lands.

So we knew, after so many decades, that some folks — a lot of folks — were frightened of the idea of wilderness, and we knew the specificity of their fears, even if we didn't agree with them or find the fears rational. But we went out anyway and challenged those people: Enough about what you don't want, or don't like, or think you don't like. What are you *for?* What *do* you want?

And like earth divers seeking to discern a buried landscape from long ago, we began constructing a map of what people wanted — in the frontcountry, in the backcountry, and even in the towns. We listened instead of trying to persuade or argue, and we drew on the map where people liked to snowmobile and places where they did not or could not. We mapped the roadless areas — the ones we know so intimately, from twenty years or more of hiking — and mapped the areas where people wanted to be able to log, and mapped the places along existing open roads where overstocked forests, usually the crowded legacy of old clearcuts, are thickest.

We mapped other community needs and desires too: sidewalks that people want in Troy, scenic rock walls along mountain roads, brick and cobble downtown streets, and the highest-priority open lands — still barely open — that the gone-away timber companies, having now turned into real estate companies, are selling.

We even sat down with the local ATV club — terrible beasts, those two-cycle engines, like chain saws on Rollerblades — and agreed to support a study aimed at finding a noncontroversial route (perhaps on old timber company lands) where they could ride, as long as it was near town and did not disturb threatened or sensitive wildlife.

And we told our traditional opponents, finally, for the ten thousandth time, what we wanted — what we needed. A big central core of wilderness in the Yaak. A big chunk of permanently protected land up in the Northwest Peaks. And something permanently protected at Mount Henry, where so many of these discussions began, so long ago — long before even the passage of the 1964 Wilderness Act.

Once not merely the proud icon of the valley but perhaps the ultimate core of wildness in the valley, the Mount Henry roadless area was nearly 600,000 acres of intact wildland, completely unfragmented. A lone family, the McIntires, homesteaded beneath its visage seventy-plus years ago. Tales of grizzly bears, mountain lions, wolverines, and woodland caribou permeate that era — the 1930s and onward — as do those of porcupines and badgers, moose and eagles. Mount Henry was a centerpiece for stories — it is still the stronghold for the last genetically pure population of inland redband trout, a kind of landlocked salmon, left in the valley — though today that 600,000 acres (an area approximately two-thirds the size of Glacier National Park) has been whittled down to a more antiseptic 13,197 acres according to Forest Service estimates.

It's in this historic core — the last of the untouched last — where we've begun our Headwaters Restoration Partnership Project, in which we're attempting to begin sewing back together that tattered landscape, trying to help create conditions that will make the land more receptive to opportunities for that earlier wildness to be breathed back into it. (And how long might it take to regain a 600,000-acre wilderness? Longer than any of us might have remaining, I fear; but it is a beautiful dream, and not unattainable in someone's life, if not ours.)

So when the YVFC took all those various pieces, laid them out on the table, and used as a backdrop this immense national forest, a narrative began to assemble itself.

We constructed a linked proposal utilizing those various pieces in which, for once, there was incentive for each side to support the other's needs; a system in which, as certain goals were met by one party, the legislative bill carried with it the goals of all the other parties.

On paper, it was so simple, after all those years of savage fighting, that it truly almost assembled itself. There were, despite some folks' previous bluster to the contrary, certain areas in the Yaak that almost everyone agreed not only were wild but should be kept wild and designated as wilderness. And by addressing those previous opponents' real fears — that they would be shut out of the areas where they had been snowmobiling for twenty years or longer, or that not only were the mills closed but there were communities and forests at risk of burning up due to wildfires of magnitudes that exceeded the fires' historic ranges — there was something for almost everyone in the bill.

And on still more common ground, everyone agreed that we had to try to find a way to protect our open space — to slow down and somehow manage the pace of new- and second-home development that was shredding the natural fabric of the landscape.

As these dialogues progressed, we brought in regional and then national environmental groups, who agreed, as we had hoped they would, that they would be far keener to support the logging of small-diameter overcrowded trees in the vicinity of homes and communities than projects in the still pristine backcountry; and that regional environmentalists would be further inspired to support logging if there were incentives such as wilderness protections in that backcountry.

It can be expensive work at times, treating an area to protect it from fire, and while the major environmental groups' budgets are stretched thin to breaking, we envisioned, and still do, that various financial resources might nonetheless find their way into such a win-win proposal, and that indeed, as we have already proven with our Headwaters Restoration Partnership Project, there can be significant job creation in repairing damaged watersheds, and that further, it is possible to help run such projects with nongovernmental dollars.

The pieces began to accrete, increasingly secure, around this surprising and novel concept of solidarity and support, which was, in the end, pretty much the only avenue any of us had left uncharted. (There had been a previous attempt at linking timber production with wilderness protection — the Kootenai-Lolo Accords of 1988, as well as a couple of wilderness bills, some decent, others abysmal, including then-Representative Pat Williams's very fine bill, which protected 154,000 acres of Yaak wildlands, and which passed the House with 302 bipartisan votes, only to be stalled by Senate stonewalling — but something, in the end, always came apart; there was always a design flaw, or a political weak point, or an untimeliness that a single enemy had always been able to exploit.)

The hope this time is that the plan is modest enough to serve as a beginning, a template, for getting along, and that by directly engaging every possible interest group, it will be more stable, able to endure the stormy weather in the halls of a U.S. Congress so very far away.

And that's pretty much how it's working. Amazingly, we've gotten our county commissioners to support this little experiment, even after, less than a few months earlier, they had gone on record as opposing any and *all* proposed wilderness for the county. This opposition gave the Kootenai National Forest's then-supervisor (who's since retired) political cover to erase all recommended wilderness from the forest planning process — wiping completely off the map, overnight, nearly a quarter-million acres of proposed wilderness, including roughly 70,000 acres in the Yaak.

Oh, the complexities, and the boredom of writing about them, and the boredom of reading about them! I'm trying to get this down, here on the eve of success, in bare-bones prose, for the historical record — passing over, like a fleeting cloud, the years of bitter meetings, the sleepless, angst-ridden nights, the elevated and then dashed hopes, and the betrayals and lies, lies told by the opposition and, worse yet, lies told or believed by those previously considered to be your allies. It is surely this way for any social movement; but finally, we are on the threshold.

Protected public lands and communities with significant land trusts are the main engines of economic health in the West these days — the figures are astounding, with 40 percent differentials in economic growth between counties that have protected open space versus those that have not — and regardless of whether a state is red or blue, the wise and vibrant ones are basically protecting everything they can while they still have the faint opportunity to do so, and are then encouraging the development of high-end, high-paying "clean industry," with workers drawn by what economists call "amenities," or what you and I would call grizzly bears and forests.

Still, in a county that for the last fifty or more years has exported more raw logs than any other in the state, and where at one point perhaps half of the population depended on logging for its livelihood (with all the mill closures of the last many years, that number is now estimated to be somewhere between 3 and 5 percent), many of the people who live here and remember the not-so-old days are not keen to see the culture subsumed by golf courses and drive-through espresso booths — and neither are the environmentalists, who continue to believe, despite the many corporate abuses of the past, that there can be, in certain places, a "good" kind of logging that not only does no harm but preserves or improves the health of the forest.

In the old days, that selective mechanism used to be wildfire, but in the areas right around people's homes and communities, that's not always a preferred option. (Nothing, of course, can fully equal the genius of wildfire; the way it not only selects the weaker, smaller trees but also recycles nutrients into the soil and creates a wealth of freestanding snags, which will serve as homes for dozens of species of cavity nesters in the coming decades, with each and every one of those species connected, in one way or another, large or small, to the continuing health of the forest and the grandness of its cycle.)

But still, in those narrow, crowded strips of forest next to homes and communities, talented loggers have been working for generations, doing work so clean and precise that someone passing by who didn't know any better would never know the area had been logged.

That kind of tidiness is not the criteria for every piece of woods — indeed, one of the hallmarks of the wild Yaak is often a clamant untidiness — but in a rural county the size of some of our northeastern states, there is definitely opportunity as well as need for this kind of showcase or stewardship logging, and there are talented local contractors capable of providing that service.

The stewardship contracting authority already exists in which certain projects can recycle revenues gotten from logging on public lands into restoration projects on the public lands. A slight tweak to that authorization — to allow for a pilot project — could direct a percentage of those revenues toward the purchase of certain high-priority tracts of the industrial timberlands that would otherwise be blasted into tiny fragments for unregulated subdivisions.

The timber company lands have been pretty much cut over, but they're productive lands capable of yielding a sustainable flow of fiber each year in the form of small-diameter trees, which in turn could be harvested for fuel in local power-generation projects. (The town of Troy loses its long-term utility contract in another year anyway.) Using these timber company lands as nurseries for fuels for schools and local power-generation fiber sources would protect the open space and would preserve wildlife habitat, including that of threatened, endangered, and sensitive species such as grizzly bears, the protection of which is a government mandate, and at times a costly, if critical, one. As such, implementation of a plan like this one would be providing a service to the rest of the country by helping accomplish this mandate.

Such a program, in addition to being managed by a local community land trust (which would take care of only the private lands, not the associated public lands, the management of which would continue to be performed by the U.S. Forest Service), could also help protect local county budgets from being drained by the obligatory servicing of far-flung rural subdivisions, which — according to studies by the University of Wyoming, and others — can cost a rural county more than twice what is brought in by the tax revenue from those developments.

Where will the money come from? That's the big question, and even though there's no money left in government these days due to the current administration's rush to war, it's a good sign at least that whenever we in the YVFC make our presentation, that's the first question folks ask: how could we ever pay for such a project?

Ironically, the wilderness — the most desired element, by our group — is the cheapest. It's free. But, at the other end of the spectrum, the purchase of those industrial timberlands — will take a huge amount of money. (It's a wise value, a wise investment, in American wilderness — an irreplaceable value — but expensive, these days, where once it was not expensive, in its rarity.)

And lying somewhere between this high cost and low cost lies the restoration piece of the puzzle, the stewardship process, tailor made for the cautious work required in the areas immediately adjacent to human communities. Not to sound like too much of a policy wonk, but the pieces, the existing authorizations, are all already there, or available with only a few of the slightest of tweaks, to make them even more place-specific, more appropriate to accomplishing the multiple tasks of fighting wildfire, protecting threatened, endangered, and sensitive species, providing local employment, creating community unity, and yielding natural resources in addition to restoring damaged landscapes.

All we have to do is hammer together a little shell of a nonprofit group, a county co-op of sorts — an investment vehicle — and we're good to go. Montana's senior senator, Max Baucus, helped pass legislation known as New Markets Tax Credits, in which approximately $15 billion — not million, but billion — is to be made available over a seven-year period to certain and select communities around the country that qualify through virtue of the most dire of economic statistics. Our portion of Lincoln County is one of only two counties in the entire state that qualifies. The credits — which can be converted to cash, if the proper investment vehicle is assembled — are ours for the taking, if we hurry. (The authorization is due to expire in three more years.) The program is extremely flexible, calls only for triple bottom-line equity to be accomplished — social, economic, and conservation goals achieved through whatever community organization implements a project aimed at hiring local folks, restoring the environment, and providing some social services as well.

Qualifying communities in the Northeast have already leapt all over this program, gobbling up almost half of that $15 billion. A typical New England–state New Markets Tax Credit program will involve the creation of a "restoration" or "challenge" or "community" forest, in which industrial timberlands are purchased, providing the conservation equity.

Firewood is sold from those lands, achieving job creation and income flow — and some of the revenue is funneled to schools, or the creation of hiking, biking, and ski paths, helping to provide social equity.

Here in Lincoln County, by partnering such a community or restoration forest with stewardship activities on the public lands adjacent to those old industrial (privately owned) timberlands, we could double our income flow, treat for wildfire dangers around human communities (producing a savings to U.S. taxpayers), protect grizzly bear habitat (providing a savings to U.S. taxpayers), provide local employment, and protect a traditional logging culture.

I've said all this before. It's a winning template for Montana, particularly at the local level, and by folding in associated wilderness protection, environmental groups who traditionally appeal and litigate timber sales would now be more motivated to support these less controversial stewardship and restoration projects. Various nongovernmental philanthropic organizations would also be inclined to funnel outside investment into the community, buying more private forest lands (industrial and nonindustrial, from willing sellers) — protecting more wildlife habitat, as well as preserving the public's traditional access to these lands — and treating more land in that fire-prone wildland-urban interface.

Doubtless there would be some merchantable timber extracted from these lands, providing more cash flow into that magic funnel, which, across the life of the investment vehicle, is authorized to provide an immediate 40 percent leverage, via tax credits, to the investors (whether philanthropic or for-profit). This yield then could be used to buy more community or restoration forest land (from the private sector, *not* from the public land base). Smaller-diameter wood from these lands could be sold as firewood, particularly to the already-existing Fuels for Schools program — a ready-made market, welcome to the eyes of any venture capitalist.

But why stop there? Even though these gnawed-over industrial timberlands are still some decades shy of being able to begin once again yielding significant (and sustainable) amounts of saw logs, those lands can be relied on to produce a certain amount of small-diameter fiber per acre per year — biomass, measured in tons rather than board feet. With nearly a million acres of industrial private timberland at large and on the selling blocks here in Lincoln County, the annual yield from those lands (most of which would need to be managed more intensively, due to their downwind proximity to the human communities) could easily power a local utility company by burning that wood in superhot, superclean conditions. Power generated in excess of the community's needs (and benefiting from still more tax credits, for generating alternative and sustainable energy) could be sold to the Bonneville Power Administration, helping facilitate the removal of the archaic salmon-killing dams along the Columbia River, and those revenues — you guessed it — could be rolled over into the local communities to help purchase, among other things, more open space, more wildlife habitat, more community or restoration forests.

We couldn't bite off the whole million acres at once, I don't think — the price tag at today's inflated golf course prices would be in excess of $1 billion (a half-day's worth of war in any oil-bearing Middle Eastern country) — but a long-term, low-interest loan could stop the liquidation and buy us time to return to a sustainable rate of logging on those lands.

We could use existing state dollars to fund a conservation area design (CAD) to prioritize in which individual timberlands to invest first.

Once the vehicle is built, and made right — once the dream is dreamed, and dreamed purely — success, and change, will be drawn to it: I am convinced of that. Further adjustments can be made to tweak the vehicle's efficiency, making it — conservation and community investment — ever more attractive to any number of disparate investors. Going back to one of our aces in the hole, Montana's senior senator, Max Baucus — the ranking Democrat on the Finance Committee — we could, in this pilot program aimed at developing new incentives for collaboration, make the model even more profitable by assigning an experimental system of tax accreditation for wood processors handling materials in these fuels-and-fire reduction zones: a tax system in which, in such a zone, it begins to make economic sense to saw down a two-inch overstocked Doug fir even when the traditional system currently draws the line of economic breakeven at, say, trees twice that large, or larger.

Even a 30 percent advantage in the tax code for fiber harvested (under strict environmental and sustainable safeguards) within a quarter-mile of communities could help make even more money flow into this Seussian, land-saving contraption. This grizzly-saving contraption. And, if it's wired right, it can also be a school-saving, community-strengthening contraption, and one that helps rescue also the independent timber industry, which by all rights should be the ally, not the opponent, of environmentalists. "Turning the *Titanic*," activists sometimes call such ambitious maneuvers, in an amusing mix of metaphors: changing the direction of something massive that is not accustomed to turning on a dime; and turning something, with similar urgency, just before it hits the iceberg. Turning something that might already have struck the iceberg.

Local and regional mills that log on these noncontroversial projects in the frontcountry can add still more value to their product by embracing a wilderness partnership with the local environmental group. Consumers — particularly home-builders — in addition to wanting quality at affordable prices, want to know the story behind the products they're purchasing: where their meat and poultry came from, where their milk came from, how it was produced, and the ecological cost, or footprint, of that production. And "wilderness wood" — lumber and finished wood products not gotten from the wilderness itself, but rather, wood that actively participated in and contributed to the first wilderness designation for public lands in the Yaak Valley, and that aids the protection of grizzly bears, employs local workers, helps fund rural schools, and reduces fire dangers to communities — well, that's one hell of a cachet, for many purchasers, given a choice.

And, once again, going to our ace in the hole, Senator

Baucus and his position on the Finance Committee, we can get tax accreditations in this pilot area — this Lincoln County project, this wilderness-and-wood project, this grizzly recovery project — for private landowners who choose to tithe their wood (or fiber) to be secured by certified personnel enrolled in the project. And once again, tax incentives could be structured to help facilitate the processing of smaller-diameter wood that might be coming off some of these overstocked private lands, as well as any extremely fine fuels — "slash" — that might be dedicated toward the local community or restoration forest's energy generation.

(Baucus has already established baseline protection for private investors in such a timberland initiative by guaranteeing that any inventory lost to wildfire can be deducted from business costs: a critical safety net for operating in this venture during an era of global warming, drought, and overstocked stands. And again, it should be noted that this tax code protection extends not just to the multinational corporations' industrial timberlands but to anyone's private property: whether a five- or ten- or fifty-acre home site, or a thousand-acre ranch. If you own trees, your baseline inventory will be protected. This makes good business sense — encourages future investment — and also provides a literal firewall against the kind of wholesale liquidation the big corporations unleashed on Montana in the 1980s, with ecological effects that communities, wildlife, and the independent wood products industry is still reeling from, decades later, in the form of tighter regulations, less management opportunity, and diminished or degraded wildlife habitat.)

We'll design a better plan, this time. Our little community group will create incentives for success rather than incentives for failure.

Just because a thing looks good on paper does not necessarily mean it will work in the world; but even though this particular plan has not been attempted anywhere in Montana or, to my knowledge, the West, there are projects elsewhere in the world that share a similar ethos. In December of 2004 I traveled to the newly democratic country of Namibia, in southern Africa, to work on a story concerning the conservation and recovery of black rhinos, as charismatic a megafauna as our continent's grizzly bear. Indeed, the stories of the two species were in many respects disturbingly similar. It's estimated that roughly 100,000 rhinos once roamed Africa, while it's believed that an equal number of grizzlies were present in the United States as recently as only two hundred years ago.

Since that time, both species have been in freefall, with the black rhinos of Namibia faring just as poorly. We may have only one or two dozen grizzlies left in the Yaak; the Kuenene region in the northwestern corner of Namibia saw its rhino numbers plummet to around five dozen.

Like the grizzly, the rhino is an enormous creature — weighing up to three thousand pounds — of enormous specialization millions of years in the making and characterized by an inability to compromise, or to accept a lessening of the wilderness qualities of its native landscape — providing, in that fashion, the gold standard for such matters. Like the grizzly, the rhino possesses a sophisticated and elegant and highly specialized, fitted connection to that native landscape, to the point where that one species not only fits, like the world's most complex and intelligent organic gearing, every other possible element of landscape and process, but is so connected to its landscape that the final removal of such a species — a grizzly, or a rhino — topples a myriad of other elements within that biotic sphere.

None among us would confuse a buffalo with any certain type of hawk, and yet take away the buffalo and gone are the grasses and prairie dogs that depended on the buffalo's particular style of grazing, and their vast recycling of nutrients; and gone too, then, is a certain seasonal wave of certain species of hawks, feeding on prairie dogs; and gone, ultimately — like an echo, or a shadow from something that passed before the sun only a century ago, or a moment ago — is the prairie itself.

These things — grizzlies, rhinos, buffaloes — were not given to us by happenstance, and though we too, in much faster fashion, have insinuated ourselves into nearly every niche, or attached ourselves, like a virus, to nearly every protuberance that the world has to offer, we lack perhaps utterly the time-tested, well-aged conviction of biological integrity. We arose quickly, like a single night's dream, and have precious little deep history or pedigree to support us, I fear, when the times, or the world (through our own making) begins to dis-assemble . . .

But I have digressed into unhappy-land, the brittle tenor

of eco-rant — the useless jeremiad, ineffective at changing anyone or anything, including even oneself, and instead only scolding, on most days, or at best sometimes making a pretty poem or an interesting essay.

Still, the world rips past, and one species after another — sometimes infinitesimal and other times grand — falls off the edge of life, as if being swept off the face of a flat-world map. Idealism is more important than ever, but so too are solutions, after nearly fifty years of failure. Increasingly, I am interested in trying not to defeat the enemy by force but instead to disarm a more muscular foe. To save wild forests, for instance, by finding a place where overstocked weedy ones could be thinned. To protect open space — private industrial timberlands — by managing them as community or restoration forests. To create power-generating co-ops through the burning of slash, in order to protect (and purchase) open space and wild country that is otherwise going under, forever, to the concrete skin of developers. To support snowmobilers — as long as wildlife concerns are met, using the best available science — who in turn support wilderness in a land that has never had any wilderness protected, and which has seen only a loss of wildness, decade after decade.

And what I saw in Africa was conservationists in a supposedly third-world country who were, in this same vein, demonstrating what is now fast becoming cutting-edge environmentalism in this country, through a concept and practice known as community-based conservation.

Most rural communities' decisions are made on the basis

of short-term economic necessities: jobs, taxes, resources. In the case of the rhinos, the solution was extraordinarily simple — to create an economic system in which a living rhino was more valuable than a dead one. The rhino conservation community instituted a program of hiring the same poachers who had been tracking and killing the rhinos, selling their horns for a bag of sugar, five pounds of coffee, a sack of flour (horns that might then be sold for twenty thousand dollars in Yemen, for use as ceremonial dagger handles, or for Chinese traditional medicine, ground into a powder used for treating the common cold), now received more money for tracking the rhinos and logging in, on handheld global positioning units, observational data and photographs, and guarding the rhinos, sometimes with the same guns they had previously used to kill them. Further, recruitment into this auxiliary guard program carried prestige, in addition to economic benefits, rather than shame and secrecy.

And from that initial success, that all-important reversal in the structure of the underlying economic paradigm, a new ethos was able to prosper. Maybe upon closer microexamination it's not so noble or artistic or elegant a blossoming — not as romantic — as one which might have been achieved through noneconomic enlightenment, but the rhino conservationists appear to have decided that with sixty rhinos left, there was no longer the indulgence of being able to endure vast centuries of stasis, or slow progress, as they waited on, and labored toward. These were often men, women, and children — the Herero people — some of whom were the descendants of prisoners of war who had been trucked out into the desert by the Germans to die, perishing usually of thirst even before any lions or leopards could find them. A few had somehow survived, though, as herders of goats now in that same pitiless desert, their existence seemed to me no more secure than when they had first been dumped into that barren land. In short, the Herero and other people hanging on at the edge of rhino country had other seemingly enduring concerns than becoming Krishna-pure tree-huggers, or, in this case, rhino-huggers. Though the Herero's numbers were slightly greater than those of the rhinos, their own existence was no less tenuous.

And however crass or inelegant or mercenary we might be conditioned to think such an approach, there have already been elegant and accruing results; for from that initial sea change, local communities are once again becoming increasingly fluent now in the concepts of ecosystem protection — conserving the landscapes and elements required to help the rhinos. In rhino country, conservation districts are developing at a rate that quite frankly exceeds and shames that of our own country's, where we remain locked, it seems, in civil strife and squabbles that are little more than luxuries or indulgences symptomatic of our temporary affluence: the culture of wasted time and wasted opportunities.

Will our plan in the Yaak have a similarly dramatic success? We believe it will. The grizzly is the slowest-reproducing land mammal native to North America; females don't bear young until around the age of six, and then the cubs — usually only one or two; but occasionally, three — remain with the mother for nearly three years. This is hardly a fast-paced life of the sort of high productivity familiar to those of us inhabiting this century's culture of machines and manufacturing, supply and demand. For me — geologist, hunter, environmentalist, logger, and, as a pretty typical American, I fear, Ur-consumer, the question comes down to one, ultimately, of personal responsibility: how badly do I want to help save this species, or this landscape, and am I willing, here at the end of the line — with maybe only ten grizzlies left in the Yaak — to partner with someone who has been defined for nearly fifty years as the enemy?

As long as it protects wilderness and grizzlies and does not betray sound science, I would partner with almost anyone at this late stage. The evidence seems clear: our little wars, in the end — however passionate — have not helped the grizzly. The new century is too huge and too hungry. We need to somehow disarm, distract, deflect, the enemy. And I think — in a backyard garden sort of way — our plan can do that.

We will be getting wilderness in the Yaak soon. I am confident of it. We have crafted an elegant if unorthodox plan. It is not enough wilderness — is really only a token amount — but we are creeping closer, have already crossed over some invisible line, some threshold, that previously separated *maybe* or *never* from certitude, from eventuality, from guarantee.

Conclusion

I COME NOW TO PERHAPS the worst of my crimes — maybe even worse than being an oil eater — which is the crime of apathy, passivity, or worse, impassivity, and its subsequent unavoidable kin, creeping despair, leavened only occasionally by the sparks of bitterness. It is the crime of weariness, and possesses also the brittle self-righteousness of believing sometimes that your heart is purer or your manners nobler than those of your opponents: for in choosing not to fight any longer, to not lie down in the mud pit of small-town fears, and to begin to serve yourself rather than a Cause, or the mountains themselves, you cross I think some threshold of scorn and arrive in the place of I-just-don't-give-a-damn-anymore. Not for the mountains, or the green summer-dusk sight of cow elk with calves trotting through the old larch and lupine, or the osprey clutching the wet shining belly of a rainbow trout, skybound — for these things you will always give a damn — but there finally comes a point in any activist's life: the dreaded burnout that you once heard about so long ago, and that you vowed never to allow to happen, as you once also before that vowed never to get old, or if you did, never to *feel* old, and most of all never to act old.

It is a survival mechanism, entering this attenuated place of waiting where, after having dreamed the dream and assembled the parts, and assisted, with your noble compatriots, in designing a plan, and then presenting it to the world and lobbying for it — beseeching, and fighting, and plotting, and beseeching again — the point at which you realize that you have done all you can do, have given your best and most honest effort every day, and every night, and that not so suddenly, life has passed you by.

The gains you have made have been incremental and intangible. Millions of dollars of small sales for local loggers, increased trust — or decreased mistrust — and increased willingness to speak of a need and desire, by an increased number of people in what was once a timber community and to some degree will always be a timber community, of the existence, logic, and values of wilderness. It's a start. A twenty-one year start.

As an ecologist and historian, I can see the fire coming — there is no way the big wildfire will not be coming, and when it does, borne on a ferocious west wind partly of the world's making and partly of its own self-generated force, it will be otherworldly, magnificent, overwhelming, and transformative; and afterward, there will be a different landscape, and a different community. All of our discussions and plans and movements in the time preceding will be rendered essentially irrelevant beyond whatever value they possessed in the moment. We will have to adapt, and look at the forest, and community, and ourselves, in a new way. And the grizzlies and other wild creatures will need even more protection, because there will be less thicket, less jungle, and instead more space and greater visibility. Less hiding cover.

This old lush dense rainforest sylvan thicket of a place may well one day seem like but a dream or fairy tale. It will be blackened, as if irradiated: and then green again. And will return again.

As an honest assessor of self, you can see how slow change is in coming. It took three decades to write and pass the Wilderness Act. Since that time, the Yaak has been waiting another four decades, going on five.

We *will* get wilderness in the Yaak. And it will be paltry: even with all our dogged and daily efforts, in no way, when wilderness comes, will it be enough. The older I get, the more I realize that all of my goals have been possessed of the crime of moderation. Even the largest of my dreams and ambitions, I realize with increasing dismay, were puny, measly, compared to the object of my dreaming. I would not say my life to date has been built overmuch of compromise, but still, it surrounds me. Many have told me that it is my passion, not my ideas, that frightens people, but if I had any of it to do over again, I would have been twice so rather than half as much. It is not so hard to be passionate and yet still remain civilized, if not dignified. There is almost always room for more passion.

I can't think of anything new to say about the Yaak other than that I love it. I can't think of any new strategies. We've invested in the logging community, schools and education, have built alliances with anglers, hunters, snowmobilers — even the ATV club agrees there should be wilderness in the Yaak! — as do many in the Forest Service, which is such a far cry from when I first came up here. The word back then, among environmentalists (who'd never been here) as well as the Forest Service itself was that the Yaak wasn't wild, that there were too many roads. Not wild? In a word: bullshit.

We have hired a new young woman who grew up here, Sarah Canepa. We could not be luckier. I so want someone to absolve me, to release me from this never-ending battle — to say, *All right, you've done enough.* I so want to step away from the encroaching bitterness of never succeeding, and of always being reviled and feared. It is not that I want the opposite of these things, to be loved and respected (at one point, I think I did), but instead, to be anonymous, as unseen and unknown and unheard — but present — as the bears or wolverines themselves.

There is no one, however, save myself who can grant me that dispensation to quit. Only the mountains themselves can authorize such retreat or retirement, and I am still waiting. And I know with sinking heart it is going to take quite a big chunk of green on the map before either the mountains or I myself will grant me that dispensation.

I can't go on, I must go on. Is this what it is like for the grizzlies, I wonder, with the little daily stresses piling up to take away their wilderness — not any one grand event, but the chipping away, the inching away, rather than the great leaps of success forward?

The road never ends, but the heart for battle wears out, as you realize more and more that your time — like a valley's wildness — may be draining away.

It is going to take bigger steps than I ever realized to keep the Yaak wild: to recover the Yaak's going-away wildness.

Even if the Yaak is kept wild, as the rest of the larger world becomes less so, then so too does the Yaak become less; for all things are still interconnected, even if often now only by memory or the echo of a once-upon-a-time design: an underlying biological integrity of fit, of possibility and yearning. Even when the systems above are wrought by fragmentation, there must surely exist a plan — an order, of design and logic — for the grace of the original wilderness below, as if coded into the rocks themselves; and coded therefore within our hearts as well, we who came up from out of the rocks, out of the dust and the clay, to be inhabited briefly by the spark of spirit.

We *will* soon see designated wilderness in the Yaak, and where for twenty-one years I have been roaring at its ridiculous absence — where has the leadership been, any leadership, within the Forest Service? where is the courage, in the

Forest Service, or anywhere? — I know I will next be roaring at the inadequacy of whatever tiny amount is offered as recompense for the long absence, the long injustice.

Still, I wonder what I will feel when we first and finally get something on the boards: when we finally take the first step in acknowledging a permanent commitment to this region, this near-mythical valley that is probably more amazing than even those of us who revere it will ever fully know. Will I allow myself one full day of relief, if not celebration; or if not one full day, six hours?

Some days, I imagine how I will spend those hours. I envision the particular mountain I will climb, and the view I will behold — transformative, in the realization that that view will forever after not be at risk of being compromised by mankind's errors. The view will change, certainly, over the decades, and the centuries — but it will not change by man's hand, but rather by nature's.

As it always has before, since the beginning of time, and the beginning of matter.

Maybe I'll even take a nap there: but then I'll get up and push on a little farther. I know the hike I'll take, when we first and finally get some wilderness on the boards. We might scratch out only 10 or 15 percent, in our first attempt, but it's been eighty-plus years since Aldo Leopold and the others began speaking of the need for primitive areas, for wilderness areas. I'll spend a part of one day celebrating the eighty-year wait.

And after that? I wonder if I will know an overwhelming frustration at how far yet we will have to go — of the way this small million acres fits, like the center heart-piece, into so much of the rest of the wild irreplaceable West. There are lines from a poem by Mary Oliver, "The Swan," that I think of occasionally.

> Said Mrs. Blake of the poet:
>
> I miss my husband's company —
>   he is so often
>   in paradise.
>   Of course! the path to heaven
>
> doesn't lie down in flat miles.
>   It's in the imagination
>   with which you perceive
>   this world,
>
> and the gestures
>   with which you honor it.
>   Oh, what will I do, what will I say, when those
>   white wings
>   touch the shore?

What will I do? Will I be able to hand the scrolled-up maps over to younger people, and to step away with honor and dispensation — with permission? For better or worse, my family — never having asked for such a thing — has been saddled with a pariah.

The new children moving to town who may not come and play with yours because your name is in the paper yet again.

The new people not knowing any better, or not possessing the courage to inquire: building lives atop a foundation of old legacy, old lies. And so on the future, and a history of place, proceeds.

I think sometimes it is exactly like this for the grizzlies, and the wolverines.

All I ever wanted to do was write short stories, novels, poems. I did not set out or desire to enter a territory where public employees and elected officials focused on me as the source of their fears, their ills, their woes. I did not mean to enter a land, a territory, where I would be identified by public servants as an attempted murder suspect simply because I love and need wilderness, or for any other reason. All I ever wanted was to write short stories. To weed the garden, to fish with the girls in our green canoe. And to be a young man, and then a middle-aged man, and then an old man, still doing these things, and nothing else.

I never wanted to go to war. And the war, I realize, will never end.

For all the setbacks, all the challenges, all the heartaches, all the fears and doubts and second-guessings — should I ever have lifted the first finger to try to help protect these mountains? I sometimes have to laugh, because even now — as a middle-aged man who's traveled irrevocably past most of that sweet green young land of drifting in the canoe without a care in the world, pursuing my own desires rather than some larger calling — even now, knowing that the war never fully ends, and knowing that to date I have half failed in a life of art, there are still mornings when, for no reason, and in the face of all supporting evidence to the contrary, I wake up feeling fresh and strong and happy, wake up almost on the verge of laughter, inspirited with hope and confidence and the belief — the knowledge — that any venture begun with and possessing a good heart, and passion, will somehow end well, even if the traveler cannot yet see or even imagine such an ending.

It is not every morning that I wake up that way, feeling strong and refreshed and confident and happy, and deeply fitted to this place and its seasons, but it is still that way sometimes; and on such mornings, infused from out of nowhere with the illogical promise or realization that everything will yet turn out all right, I realize that this is so even though I am not being granted the dispensation I have been looking for these last many years — permission to turn away, and take a rest — but that instead I am receiving a far more valuable dispensation, the permission and authorization to keep on going. This is not the life I would ever have chosen — not in a million years — but it is the life in which I have found myself, sidetracked, as if lost, as if stumbling, while lost, into some remote and hidden valley; and for all my continued longings, it is still not all a bad life, is in fact quite satisfying.

On good green mornings in the Yaak, I can still remember this.

How You Can Help

THERE ARE ANY NUMBER of ways you can help work to protect the last roadless areas of the Yaak. Something anyone can do — and which would be hugely helpful — is to send a short and simple letter to each of the addresses listed below, stating your desire for the last roadless lands in the Yaak Valley to be designated as wilderness. That's all the letter has to say. If you want to give your reasons, and wax eloquent, that's wonderful: but the important thing is to just send the basic message. Best of all is if you have a relationship with any of the Montana delegation — Senator Max Baucus and Senator Jon Tester, and Representative Dennis Rehberg — so that you may include the Yaak's needs in your dialogue with the congressmen. You might reside out of state, but if you do, don't let that prohibit you from contacting the delegation; these are public lands, your lands, over which the aforementioned delegation simply holds some degree of informal stewardship. Certainly, please contact your own senators and representatives as well.

You can stay in touch with the Yaak Valley Forest Council by visiting us at www.yaakvalley.org, or e-mailing us at info@yaakvalley.org.

And as a tax-exempt, 501-(C)-3 nonprofit community service organization, the YVFC would of course benefit from monetary donations that help staff the office, and from the generous and creative contributions of other goods and services and talents, as the giver sees fit. They're doing good work — the best — on the front lines of American conservation. Thanks for your help.

Please send a copy of your letter to the following:

Senator Max Baucus
511 Hart Senate Office Bldg.
Washington, D.C. 20510
www.baucus.senate.gov

Senator Jon Tester
Dirksen Senate Office Bldg.
Suite 40E, U.S. Senate
Washington, D.C. 20510
www.Tester.Senate.gov

Representative Dennis Rehberg
516 Cannon House Bldg.
Washington, D.C. 20515
www.house.gov/rehberg

Yaak Valley Forest Council
155 Riverview
Troy, MT 59935
www.yaakvalley.org

Acknowledgments

FOR A LONG TIME, I have dreaded trying to assemble an acknowledgment or thank-you list for the people who have given not just their hearts to the Yaak but their skills, talents, influence, intelligence, imagination, and all the other resources available to them. Terrified that I might leave someone out — certain that I will — I nonetheless have decided that it is better to attempt to construct a list of thank-yous and fail in part than to be certain, through my caution, of overlooking everyone.

I also feel like apologizing to the reader who might have picked up this book hoping, perhaps, for lyrical descriptions of a fantastic and mythic landscape, only to find a disproportionate amount of caterwauling. Again, this is a personal decision I've made, as a writer: given the value of what is still at stake in the Yaak, and the forces — both active and inert — that have traditionally conspired against the Yaak, it would be irresponsible at this point in time not to caterwaul. It would be nice and easy to crack wise about the situation, but at this late date even irony seems complicit with the problem: the absence of permanent commitment, via wilderness designation, to the Yaak's last wild places.

The Round River Crew — Dennis Sizemore and Trent Alvey, Brooke and Terry Tempest Williams, Doug and Andrea Peacock, Doug and Anna Milek, Chris and Katherine Filardi, Michael Soule, John Ward, John Wickersham, Bruce Baizel and family, Jim Tolisano, Kim Heineman, Mike Magee, Julian Griggs, Chuck Rumsey, and staff and students, past, present, and future — has been inspirational both with regard to specific counsel as well as exemplars in reminding us all daily why, and how much, wilderness matters.

The activist and journalist Steve Thompson helped us from the very beginning with organizational advice — he's one of the YVFC's godfathers, in that regard — as did Jim Owens of the Brainerd Foundation. Thanks to statewide and regional conservation organizations and the individuals who serve them, such as American Wildlands, Y2Y (especially Katie Deuel and Elizabeth White), Cabinet Resources Group (Bill Martin, Cesar Hernandez, Doug Ferrell, Judy Hutchins, Diane Mosley, Cal and Irene Ryder, and others), the Montana Wildlife Federation (in particular Tom France), the Wilderness Society (particularly Bob Ekey), the Montana Chapter of Trout Unlimited (directed ably by Bruce Farling), the national chapter of Trout Unlimited (likewise inspirited by Chris Wood), Louisa Willcox and the Natural Resources Defense Council, Bob Clark of the Sierra Club, Steve and Cristina Eisenberg, Todd Tanner and Molly McCabe, Carl

Pope, Tim Mahoney, Jim Posewitz of the Cinnabar Foundation, Joel Webster of the Theodore Roosevelt Conservation Partnership, Ben Alexander and Ray Rasker, the Kootenai River Network, YVFC board members and staff — Scott Daily, Sue Janssen, Mary Campbell, Pam Fuqua, David and Darla Henderson, Sarah Canepa, Tony Johnson, Tim and Joanne Linehan, and Jimmy Marten.

Checks of another nature — cold hard cash on the barrelhead — have allowed us to hire our amazing executive director, our wonderful local place-based staff, and our keen-eyed and passionate Forest Watch coordinator, while also conducting more than a million dollars' worth of environmental repairs to degraded watersheds in the upper Yaak, using local workers. I'm grateful to the following organizations for their financial assistance in these projects: the 444S Foundation, Acorn Foundation/Common Council, American Fisheries (Montana Chapter), Arthur B. Schultz Foundation, Ben & Jerry's Foundation, Brainerd Foundation, Bullitt Foundation, Bunting Family Foundation, Cabinet Resources Group, Kendall Foundation, Cadeau Foundation, Campion Foundation, Cinnabar Foundation, Liz Claiborne/Art Ortenberg Foundation, Duke University, Engelhard Foundation, Ferguson Foundation, Forever Wild Foundation, Fund for Wild Nature, Gordon Hamersley, Idaho Panhandle Chapter of Trout Unlimited, Kongsgaard Goldman Foundation, Kootenai Valley Trout Club, Lannan Foundation, the Lincoln County Resource Advisory Council, the Lyons Press, Maki Foundation, Matthew Hansen Foundation, Montana Arts Council, Montana Committee for the Humanities, Montana Fish Wildlife and Parks, Future Fisheries Project, Montana Shares, Montana Trout Foundation, Montana Wilderness Association, Montana Chapter of the Sierra Club, Nasaw Family Foundation, National Forest Foundation, New Land Foundation, Bill Newsom, Norcross Foundation, Northern Environmental Support Trust, Patagonia, Peradam Foundation, Pew Charitable Trust, Resources for Community Collaboration, Kevin Rowell, Ruth Mott Fund, Sandy Hollow Arts & Recreation for the Environment, Tides Foundation, Training Resources for the Environmental Community, the Trout and Salmon Foundation, Trout Unlimited (Flathead Chapter), Wilburforce, the Writer's Voice, and the Y2Y Initiative.

I'm grateful to Project Lighthawk, the "Environmental Air Force," for the dozens of flyovers they've provided for media, politicians, and local people interested in getting an invaluable bird's-eye view of this unique land and the cumulative effects of past management decisions.

Jim Burchfield at the University of Montana School of Forestry, Kira Finkler with Trout Unlimited, George Wuerthner, Dan Crockett and David Stallings, formerly with Rocky Mountain Elk Foundation, have helped whenever asked, across the years, as has Tim Mahoney, with Campaign for America's Wilderness.

Early-days local Yaak activists such as Chip Clark, Bob Zimmerman, Dave Erickson, Don Clark, Maria Frasier, and — going way back — Jeannette McIntire have provided a template for the responsibility of giving local voice to one's needs in a climate where the exercise of free speech was nonetheless certain to bring significant ostracizing.

Past members of Montana Wilderness Association — Bob Decker, Paul Edwards, Ross Rodgers, Leeann Drabenstott, Karole Lee, Susan Bryan, Ross Titus, Roger Sherman, Gerry Jennings, Jill Duryee, Kendall Flint and Kate Saako, John Adams, and many others — have also remained steadfast supporters of the need to protect the Yaak's wild places, even though these individuals live far away in this vast state. John Gatchell and Tim Baker likewise continue to stay updated with our local community-based efforts, and we're confident that when a Montana wilderness bill is finally passed, the Yaak will be well represented, finally.

In 1997, the Orion Society's Forgotten Language Tour gave our small local voice a much-needed boost when four nationally acclaimed writers — Richard Nelson, Robert Michael Pyle, Janisse Ray, and Terry Tempest Williams — spent the better part of a week in Lincoln County, visiting the schools and mills and giving public readings.

In 1999, the phenomenal puppeteer Beth Nixon performed for the YVFC's and the community's benefit an unforgettable "Puppet Extravaganza," which was reprised in 2007.

For many years, Marc and Tara Morrison have serviced an independent website dedicated to the Yaak's roadless areas (www.geocities.com/RainForest/Vines/5054). The painter and publisher Russell Chatham has remained a staunch supporter, as have the photographers Randy Beacham and Donald M. Jones.

In the absolutely critical arena of politics, we have received, at various times, useful advice and encouragement and audience from Tracy Stone-Manning and Matt Jennings in Senator Jon Tester's office, daily wisdom and inspiration from Rebecca Manna, Karen Bridges, and Governor Brian Schweitzer and his staff — Hal Harper, Mike Volesky, Evan Barrett, Pamela Cote. Also helpful in this area were Charlie Wright, Rosalie Cates, and Craig Rawlings, and the Lincoln County commissioners John Konzen and Marianne Roose, who have called for common-ground solutions, along with local politicians such as Eileen Carney; Mary Frances Repko in Senator Feingold's office; Amelia Jenkins and Rick Healy in Representative Rahall's office; Matt Jones, Paul Wilkins, Kirby Campbell-Rierson, and Meladee Haynes in Senator Baucus's office; Art Noonan, Jim Foley, and, indefatigably, the former Montana representative Pat Williams.

I'd like to believe that the national elections of 2006 — in which to some degree the state of Montana came to be seen as a bellwether, having two years previously voted in a Democratic governor while at the same time unfortunately (in my personal opinion) voting overwhelmingly for George W. Bush, making it one of the reddest states in the Union, at that time — were the beginning of a new day, a second chance, for the wilderness areas throughout not just Montana but the West. Something must have been working just beneath the surface, for in Montana in 2006, Governor Schweitzer was elected, and two years later, at a national scale, we saw that thing — a clamant desire for something better, and a disgust with the arrogance and corruption — begin to emerge.

Prior to the 2006 elections, the YVFC had been working not only with Montana's Democratic (and senior) senator Max Baucus, but with the state's Republican senator, Conrad Burns, who at that time was chair of the powerful Senate Appropriations Committee. Dissatisfied with Burns and inspired by the candidacy of the Democrat Jon Tester, Montana voters voted against Burns and for Tester, who won by 3,562 votes, giving the national Democratic Party their fifty-first senator, allowing them to regain the majority nationally by that margin of 3,562 Montana votes, and subsequently allowing the Congress to convene hearings on the myriad governmental irregularities that had been proceeding apace prior to those historic elections.

Tracy McIntyre with the Lincoln County Economic Development office has been supportive, as has Pat Pezelle, former president of Flathead Valley Community College; Gary Blaz, former superintendent of Eureka Public Schools; the Libby Rod and Gun Club; and the late Roger Morris, former *Western News* editor. Local snowmobile club president Jerry Wandler is acknowledged, along with the Lincoln County Ridge Riders president, Joel Chandler. The visionary courage of mill owners such as Doug Chapel of Chapel Cedar in Troy and Loren Rose at Pyramid Lumber in Seeley Lake is also much appreciated, as is that of Troy logger Kurt Rayson and stewardship contractor Wayne Hirst. Former Three Rivers district rangers Mike Balboni and Mike Herrin brought civility to the dialogue over the need for dispersed Yaak wilderness. Ralph Stever of the Lincoln County Chemical Dependency Program has been a fantastic partner with help in facilitating and sponsoring or cosponsoring numerous community activities and presentations, and we're grateful also to area specialists who have given lectures in our Community Conversations series: the mycologist Larry Evans, the archeologist Becky Timmons, Cindy Swanson, Ed Nusselroad, Dale Bosworth, Gail Kimbell, Kathy McAllister, and former U.S. Forest Service chief Mike Donbeck.

The Yaak Wilderness Festival (www.yaakvalley.org) is held around the last Saturday of July or first Saturday in August of each year, and each year receives great labor and support from folks such as Patti O'Bryan and Scott Daily, the Dirty Shame Saloon, Wayne Kasworm, Jerry Brown, and musicians such as the Alan Lane Band, Sol Jibe, Frank Chiavarini and the Live Wire Choir, Amy Martin, Ben Weaver, the Broken Valley Road Show, Hey Dan Rhythm Band, Earth Sister Rhythm, JD Smith and the Three Legged Dog, the Edwards Park Band, Greg Denning, and Melefluent.

In Montana, the Trust for Public Land, led by Eric Love, and the Montana Land Reliance, led by Amy Eaton O'Herren and the Vital Ground Foundation, have also committed to protecting and preserving the special qualities that help make up the Yaak's uniqueness, while also working to retain the production of sustainable fiber on private lands.

Editors such as Doug Barasch at Natural Resource Defense Council's *OnEarth* magazine, David Seideman and Roger Cohn at *Audubon* magazine, Monika Bauerlein at *Mother Jones,* Joan Hamilton at *Sierra,* Janet Duckworth at the *Los Angeles Times,* Mike England at *Outside Bozeman,* Alan Weltzien, Ann St. Clair, Don Burgess, Gordon Lish, and Dorothee Kocks of *Wasatch Journal,* Allen Jones and Seabring Davis at *Big Sky Journal,* Jennifer Sahn and Chip Blake at *Orion,* Camille Hykes at *Tricycle,* Valerie Harms at *Distinctly Montana,* Patricia Marshall at *Forest,* Emilie Buchwald at *Milkweed,* Barbara Ras at the University of Georgia Press, and Scott Slovic and Mike Branch have all been supportive in spirit as well as content of Yaak writings. In 2002, the Lyons Press published an anthology of writings about the Yaak, *The Roadless Yaak,* in which thirty-five different writers and scientists visited the Yaak, then wrote about it, in efforts to destigmatize the notion that mine was the only voice interested in seeing this unique ecosystem protected. For this, I will forever be grateful to Sandra Alcosser, Bob Butz, Doug Chadwick, Scott Daily, Alison Hawthorne Deming, Mike Dombeck, David James Duncan, Amy Edmonds, Jeff Ferderer, Jim Fergus, Tom Franklin, Debra Gwartney, Sue Halpern, Bill Kittredge, Carolyn Kremers, Laurie Lane-Zucker, Bob Love, Tim Linehan, Gregory McNamee, Bill McKibben, Ellen Meloy, Roy Parvin, Robert Michael Pyle, Doug Peacock, Janisse Ray, Pattiann Rogers, Lynn Sainsbury, Laura Sedler, Bob Shacochis, Annick Smith, Todd Tanner, Steve Thompson, John Wickersham, Terry Tempest Williams, and Chris Wood.

Editorial assistance has been provided for years by Will Vincent, Susanna Brougham, and Alison Kerr Miller at Houghton Mifflin, and the late Harry Foster; I'm hugely grateful to them for work on *Why I Came West,* and to Florian Schultz for the jacket photo, and to Bob Overholtzer for the book design.

The Yaak has benefited from the generous and inspired media outreach work of Ben Long of Resource Media Specialists, Ross Rademacher of Maverick Marketing, the journalism of Dick Manning (author of, among other fine books, the Montana classic *Last Stand*), and the advice and support of Roy and Susan O'Connor, Tom Campion of Zumiez, and Peter Metcalfe of Black Diamond, and Robert Redford of the Sundance Institute.

I'm grateful to my family. Only they know the full tally of hours gone by.

In the end, then, it comes down to this: am I a glutton? For my initial response in looking back over this surely partial list of thank-you's is one of the cup being half empty, rather than half full. All this work, all this support, all this goodwill, and still we have no designated wilderness in the Yaak Valley? You can't help but think, *What if I had never arrived here, or what if I had never lifted a finger? How would things be any different?*

Maybe this year. Maybe this is the year. Please turn to page 225, and consider what you might do to help, in ways both traditional or perhaps more creative and nontraditional. Surely we are getting closer.